BALLOONS

AND

AIRSHIPS

BALLOONS
AND
AIRSHIPS

A Tale of Lighter Than Air Aviation

Anthony Burton

PEN & SWORD
TRANSPORT
AN IMPRINT OF PEN & SWORD BOOKS LTD.
YORKSHIRE – PHILADELPHIA

First published in Great Britain in 2019 by
Pen and Sword Transport
An imprint of
Pen & Sword Books Ltd
Yorkshire - Philadelphia

ISBN 978 1 52671 949 2

Typeset in 10.5/13.5 pt Palatino
Typeset by Aura Technology and Software Services, India
Printed and bound in India by Replika Press Pvt. Ltd.

Pen & Sword Books Ltd incorporates the Imprints of Pen & Sword Books Archaeology, Atlas, Aviation, Battleground, Discovery, Family History, History, Maritime, Military, Naval, Politics, Railways, Select, Transport, True Crime, Fiction, Frontline Books, Leo Cooper, Praetorian Press, Seaforth Publishing, Wharncliffe and White Owl.

For a complete list of Pen & Sword titles please contact

PEN & SWORD BOOKS LIMITED
47 Church Street, Barnsley, South Yorkshire, S70 2AS, England
E-mail: enquiries@pen-and-sword.co.uk
Website: www.pen-and-sword.co.uk

Or
PEN AND SWORD BOOKS
1950 Lawrence Rd, Havertown, PA 19083, USA
E-mail: Uspen-and-sword@casematepublishers.com
Website: www.penandswordbooks.com

Contents

CHAPTER ONE

Taking to the Air

Man it seems has always dreamed of flying. Every culture has stories of unlikely winged creatures, from the angels of Judaic and Christian tradition to the feathered gods of the Aztecs. There are even stories of flying machines being built in the ancient world, such as the vimanas of India, mentions of which were found in a Sanskrit manuscript – though it didn't surface until the nineteenth century. These amazing machines were said to be capable of great speeds and of travelling off to distant planets. Mythology also has its stories of human attempts to take to the skies, of which the most famous is the story of Icarus. He tried to fly with feathery wings held together with wax but became overconfident. He flew too near the sun, the wax melted and he plunged to his death. All these stories are very ancient, but it is not until much later that we find actual attempts by real people to emulate the birds.

Factual accounts are rather scarce, but it seems all the earliest attempts at flying involved an Icarus-like idea of making wings, sometimes even using bird feathers and then launching into the air from some high building or cliff, usually with spectacularly bad results for would-be aviators. The Chinese appear to have started things off, when the Emperor Wang Mang ordered one of his men to don wings and leap from a tower in the first century AD and he is reported as having glided down covering 100 yards on the ground, rather more a controlled fall than an actual flight. In the sixth century another Chinese emperor repeated the experiment with another of his servants: there are no records of these gentlemen trying out their own inventions.

Europeans were a little slower in developing a taste for feathered leaps from towers. The most successful attempt happened at Cordova in Al-Andalus in the ninth century. Abbas Ibn Firnas studied science and developed some form of flying machine, of which no details are known, but he was able to take off from a hilltop in 875 and reports say he remained aloft for an impressive ten minutes. Unfortunately, the landing was less successful and he injured his back quite severely and never attempted another flight. In England, the honour, if that is the word, of attempting to fly goes

The Montgolfier brothers were the first to manufacture hot air balloons, and on their public flights they made sure they were not ignored by decking them out in bright colours.

FIGURE EXACTE ET PROPORTIONS.

DU GLOBE AËROSTATIQUE,

Qui, le premier, a enlevé

des Hommes dans les Airs.

Hauteur du Globe............... 70 piéds   Poids du Globe................ 1600 Liv.
Diametre....................... 46 piéds   Poids qu'il a enlevé 16. à 1700 Liv.
Capacité..... 60000 piéds cubes   La Gallerie avoit 3. piéds de largeur.

La partie supérieure étoit entourée de Fleurs-de-lys; au-dessous les 12 Signes du Zodiaque.
Au milieu les Chiffres du Roi, entremêlés de Soleils.
Le bas, étoit garni de Mascarons et de Guirlandes; plusieurs Aigles à ailes éployées
paroissoient suporter en l'air cette puissante Machine).
Tous ces ornemens étoient de couleur d'or sur un beau fond bleu, ensorte que ce su-
perbe Globe paroissoit être d'or et d'azur.
La Gallerie circulaire, dans laquelle on voyoit M. le Marquis D'ARLANDES et
M. PILATRE DE ROZIER, étoit peinte en Draperies cramoisi à franges d'or.

Grande Notice 1786

to a monk of Malmesbury Abbey. The flight was recorded in a work written by William of Malmesbury, and tells how a young monk, Elmer, watched jackdaws flying round the abbey and gliding on air currents. He felt that if equipped with wings he could do the same – actual details of his wings were not recorded. But the records do show that in 1010 he leapt off a tower – the present abbey had not yet been built – and glided for some 200 yards before crashing and breaking both his legs. He considered another attempt, this time with a tail for stability, but the Abbot forbade it and that brought attempts at gliding off towers to an end until the sixteenth century, when there was a brief revival. In 1507, John Damain jumped from the walls of Stirling Castle with the predictably disastrous result, which he blamed on using chicken instead of eagle feathers.

There were various attempts during the Renaissance to invent flying machines, notably by Leonard da Vinci, who wrote about and sketched many different versions including an early version with a rotary screw, a sort of primitive helicopter. None was actually put to the test; the problem was the one that had plagued all early would-be aeronauts: a lack of appropriate power. Unlike birds, the muscles of Homo Sapiens are not adapted for flight. How was man to get off the ground? The answer already existed in China and had done so since at least the third century BC, when they made flying lanterns, devices we still have today and simply know as Chinese lanterns. A small lamp is placed at the bottom of a paper balloon and as the air in the balloon heats up, it rises because the hot air is lighter than the surrounding atmospheric air. Chinese lanterns are simply small hot air balloons. The idea was first shown in Europe by a priest, Bartolomeu de Gusmão, who made a paper balloon with a light underneath and demonstrated it lifting in the air at the royal court in Lisbon in 1709. No one seems to have thought that a larger version might fly with a human passenger. That vital step had to wait until nearly at the end of the 18th century and the work of the most famous men in ballooning history, Joseph-Michael and Jacques-Etienne Montgolfier.

The Montgolfier family had a long tradition of paper making. The process had first been developed in the Far East, but by the Middle Ages had reached as far as Damascus. One of the Montgolfier family was captured during the sixth crusade, a misfortune that actually helped establish the family's fortune, for it was during this time that he learned the secrets of paper manufacture. Once he was freed he returned to the family home at Ambert in the Auvergne in 1386 where he built a paper mill. He was followed by others and the local river was soon supporting a chain of mills, one of which still survives, working just as it was in the fourteenth century, with a waterwheel supplying the power. In 1693 two Montgolfier brothers, Michael and Raymond, married the two daughters of Antoine Schelle who owned mills in Annonay some 70 miles from Ambert, which the Montgolfiers soon turned to paper making. This was a decisive moment in their fortunes. The mills prospered to such an extent that they were able to add the proud claim of being officially

The Charles brothers took different path from that followed by the Mongolfiers, by using hydrogen to fill their balloon instead of hot air.

PREMIER VOYAGE AÉRIEN EXÉCUTÉ DANS UN AÉROSTAT À GAZ HYDROGÈNE PAR CHARLES ET ROBERT, Le 1er Déc.1783. DÉPART DES TUILERIES.

royal manufacturers. By the middle of the eighteenth century, control had passed to Pierre Montgolfier, and it was his two sons, Joseph, born in 1740 and Etienne, five years later, who were to add fame to fortune.

Joseph left school to go to Paris, where he became interested in all the latest scientific work that was being published there, including the English chemist Joseph Priestley's experiments with gases, which included isolating oxygen from air. He was also aware of Henry Cavendish's discovery of hydrogen. After a short time, he was called back to Annonay to help run the family business. He attempted to introduce new technology, but his father, perhaps reluctant to have a highly successful business being used for his son's experiments, preferred to set him up on his own. It seems to have been a wise decision, as Joseph's business was soon floundering in debt. Etienne was more conservative than his elder brother. He trained as an architect, but also showed an interest in physical science. When the father retired it was Etienne, then aged thirty, who took the business over and proved to be a success. Exactly what made the brothers turn to ballooning is uncertain. Popular mythology has it that Joseph saw his mother's chemise drying by the fire, when it became loose and drifted up to the ceiling. For some reason popular histories always like such romantic stories of happy accidents. So they have James Watt inventing the steam engine because he saw a kettle boiling and lifting the lid: when the more mundane story is that he was attempting to improve an earlier form of steam engine. The story of the chemise is almost certainly pure fiction.

The truth is we know very little about the brothers' early experiments or the theories on which they based them. What we do know is that they began experiments with model balloons. Joseph Black had suggested that hydrogen could be used to fill a balloon, but never made the experiment himself. Tiberius Cavallo, who wrote the first ever book on aeronautics, *History and Practice of Aerostation,* published in 1785, took up Black's idea but the material he used was too dense and the best he could manage was to create hydrogen-filled soap bubbles. There is some evidence that Joseph Montgolfier made a few attempts at making a hydrogen balloon, but he had problems making the gas in sufficient quantity and, when it was made, preventing it leaking out through the balloon fabric, whether made of paper or silk. There are also versions that suggest they made experiments using steam as the lifting agent, but as skilled paper makers they would surely have known that the best they could expect would be a soggy mass of fabric. What we can say with certainty is that the brothers experimented with heating the air inside the balloon and that this worked, though as with all early experimenters, there would be a number of failures along the way.

Although we know that when air is heated it expands; in modern scientific terms the molecules move further apart, so that any particular volume of air will then contain fewer of them and thus be lighter. Joseph Montgolfier was aware of the effect but seems to have believed that in heating it was the nature of the gases given off that caused it, and different materials were needed in the fire to get the best effect. He decided that chopped wool and damp straw were the perfect fuels. In fact, this was probably a very sensible mixture to use, even if the reasoning was faulty; the wool would burn but the damp straw would ensure that it didn't flair up and risk igniting the balloon. In later experiments they tried even odder agents, adding old shoes and decomposing meat to the mixture.

Joseph Montgolfier was convinced that ballooning had an important role to play in world affairs. In 1782 Gibraltar was under siege by combined French and Spanish forces, but the British garrison could not be dislodged. Joseph was sure he had the answer; send in troops by balloon: 'It will be possible to introduce into Gibraltar an entire army, which, borne by the wind, will enter above the heads of the English.' This was rather an ambitious statement given that no one had yet flown in a balloon at all, let alone a whole army. It was, of course, totally impractical. There was no way of steering balloons, and even if they all reached Gibraltar, they could only land in ones and twos, making it an easy task for the defenders to deal with them. Not surprisingly, his offer was not taken up by the military. Shortly afterwards it all became irrelevant as the besieged British garrison was relieved by a rather more conventional fleet under Admiral Howe.

But 1782, though it did not launch an airborne armada, did see the launch of the first Montgolfier balloon. It was a modest affair, a small envelope of silk with an opening at the bottom. But when burning paper was held beneath the aperture, the balloon inflated and rose to the ceiling of Joseph's apartment in Avignon. Encouraged by this experiment, he returned to Annonay where he repeated the experiment outdoors, with his brother as spectator. Etienne was thrilled by the experience and decided to join his brother in taking the experiments on to the next stage. They were ready to start building far larger balloons, the first of which had a capacity of about 650 cubic feet (18 cubic metres) and rose to a height of about 200 metres. A second, even larger, balloon was tried and when it came to the third version, we have details from Cavallo's history of early aeronautics.

Engraved for the European Magazine.

The Descent of the Air Balloon.

Monsieur de Montgolfiers Air Balloon, after having Ascended an Amazeing heighth above the Clouds & being Carryed in the Air 45 Leagues, fell down near a Cottage, where the poor Country People were excedingly frightend & Astonishd, the Cock, Sheep & the Duck, Came out of the Basket which had been tyed to it, unhurt.

Publish'd Dec.r 1.t 1783 by J. Fielding. Pater Noster-Row.

The early balloons were such a novelty that when they landed in rural communities they caused something of a panic. In this cartoon of the period, a priest is exorcising the demons who have descended from the skies.

The first balloon had been in the shape of a parallelepiped, in other works it looked rather like an oblong box that had been pulled around and forced out of shape. But Cavallo tells us that this balloon had a diameter of 35 feet, so it was obviously either round or slightly plum-shaped. The skin consisted of cloth and paper. It was an impressive object and was said to be able to carry a load of 450 lbs. Strong winds delayed the launch but on 25 April 1783 it was released, rose to a height of some 300 metres and was eventually found a kilometre from the launch site. The time had now come for an even more ambitious project. This time the description of the construction came from Etienne himself, so can reasonably considered as the first accurate account we have of the making of a hot air balloon. This balloon was spherical and 110 feet in circumference. It was made out of cloth lined with paper and the different sections held together by buttons and button holes.

When the monster was being inflated, two men were given the rather unenviable task of supervising the inflation and ensuring that the whole contraption did not go up in flames. As it gradually expanded to its full spherical shape, it needed eight other men to hold it to the ground. Once they let go, it sped skywards and reached a height of around 1800 metres and then drifted off with the wind. This must have come as a shock to the onlookers – and it still comes as a surprise when making a first balloon flight to find oneself shooting up like a cork from a champagne bottle. It was not an especially long flight for such a large balloon, coming to earth just ten minutes later a mere two and a half kilometres from the launch site. Etienne declared that the problem was caused by leakage through the arrays of buttonholes. This must have been a spectacular event and inevitably word eventually reached Paris, where the scientific community greeted it with scepticism. In part this may have been down to simple pique to find that two men with no official qualifications from a provincial town could achieve anything on this scale. But it also went against the firmly established 'scientific' view that heating air would not send a balloon of this size skywards; the effect could only be achieved by filling it with a lighter gas, preferably hydrogen, the lightest of all the elements.

Once something as original as a balloon flight has been achieved, it is inevitable that others will sit up, take notice and try either to replicate the event or to go one better. Jacques Charles, together with his brothers Ainé and Cadet came up with a proposal for a hydrogen balloon. He suggested using a fabric consisting of silk coated with rubber solution to keep in the gas, which was indeed an effective answer to the problem that had baffled the Montgolfier brothers. His plans for a hydrogen balloon received the active support of one of France's leading scientists, Faujas de Saint-Fond. Although originally trained as a lawyer, his real interest was in the natural world and in particular in the newly developing science of geology. He made a detailed study of volcanoes and was the first to recognise that the famous basalt pillars at the entrance to Fingal's Cave on Staffa were the result of volcanic activity. He was appointed by Louis XVI to the post of naturalist at the natural history museum in Paris, and was later given the lucrative appointment of king's commissioner for the inspection of mines and factories. With such a distinguished patron, Charles had little trouble in obtaining the finance for his experiments. A public subscription was raised with the incentive that anyone investing the minimum of one crown would be invited to watch the ascent.

The problem of preventing the hydrogen diffusing through the balloon's fabric may have been solved but producing the gas and getting it into the envelope proved altogether more troublesome. The hydrogen was manufactured from iron filings and sulphuric acid and although this was a much smaller balloon than the Montgolfier monster – a mere 12 foot in diameter – it still required almost 500 pounds of acid and 1,000 pounds of iron to produce sufficient gas. Work started early on the morning of 23 August 1783 at Charles' workshop at Place des Victoires in Paris. The iron and acid were mixed in a series of lead lined boxes, linked to the balloon by a series of pipes. Unfortunately, most of the gas simply leaked away, so a new arrangement was tried in which the gas was collected in a barrel, from which a single pipe connected to the balloon. This solved most of the leakage problem, but adding acid to iron is an exothermic reaction, in other words it generates a lot of heat. In order to stop the fabric catching fire, the balloon had to be constantly doused in water. It may have cooled the balloon, but a lot of water vapour was making its way into the balloon, where it condensed. By nine o'clock that night it was decided to abandon attempts of launching the balloon for the day.

The following morning things were looking good, in that the balloon had held its shape, but optimism was soon dashed. It turned out that there was a leak somewhere and a great deal of air had now got in as well as the hydrogen. The whole of that day was spent refilling the balloon with gas so that the first attempt at an ascent could be made first thing the following morning. At 6 a.m. the balloon, safely tethered, was allowed to rise into the air so that Charles could make some measurements. He had calculated it should have been able to lift 35 pounds, but when he tried the experiment it only managed 21 pounds and by the end of the day that had reduced to 18 pounds. Clearly gas was escaping somehow, but he was not sure quite how or why. The answer was that some acid fumes were being carried over along with the hydrogen, weakening the fabric.

Nevertheless, the balloon would lift and when it was released from its mooring, still attached to a long rope, it rose to a height of a hundred feet. The sight of a balloon suddenly appearing above the streets of Paris caused huge excitement, and crowds rushed to the scene, many of them trying to force their way into the yard at the Charles works. Fortunately, no one actually got in – but the thought of a mob crashing about round the yard with its quantities of dangerous acid, not to mention the harm that could have been done to the fragile balloon was alarming. As a result, it was decided to move the site of the first attempted ascent from the constricted Place des Victoires to the spacious Champ de Mars, a large area of parkland that gets its name from the Ecole Militaire at one end, but is best known these days for the Eiffel Tower at the other. But worried that even the appearance of the balloon being moved might draw a crowd, it was transported to the new location in the early hours of the morning with a police escort. Faujas de Saint-Fond described the scene.

'No more wonderful scene could be imagined than the Balloon being thus conveyed, preceded by lighted torches, surrounded by a 'cortege' and escorted by a detachment of foot and horse guards; the nocturnal march, the form and capacity of the body, carried with so much precaution; the silence that reigned, the unseasonable hour, all tended to give a singularity and mystery truly imposing to all those who were acquainted with the cause. The cab-drivers on the road were so astonished that they were impelled to stop their carriages, and to kneel humbly, hat in hand, whilst the procession was passing.

The ascent had been planned for 27 August, but because the balloon had to be topped up with extra hydrogen, the flight was delayed until the following day. The area was cordoned off and only ticket holders were allowed into the enclosure to watch the event. Those who couldn't get tickets found places to perch with a view over the Champ de Mars and waited for the great moment to arrive. A cannon was fired, the balloon was released and soared to a height of some 1,000 metres and drifted away across the rooftops of Paris. It eventually came down at the village of Gonesse, fifteen miles to the north of the city. It was said that the villagers assuming some strange monster was invading them, attacked the balloon and completely destroyed it. The theme of villagers horrified by the arrival of a balloon among them became a favourite with cartoonists of the day.

The government reacted to the situation by issuing an official proclamation to the effect that lighter than air balloons were being tested in France but although there were to be more experiments on a larger scale, there was no need for panic. Anyone seeing one should realise that it is not 'an alarming phenomenon, it is only a machine, made of taffeta, or light canvas covered with paper, that cannot possibly cause any harm, and which will some day prove useful to the wants of society'.

With official approval for more and larger experiments, there were now two rival camps each eager to demonstrate the superiority of their device; the hot air balloon and the hydrogen balloon. The Montgolfiers were now eager to improve on their version. They joined forces with a wallpaper manufacturer, Jean-Baptiste Réveillon who had a factory at Faubourg St. Antoine. The new balloon was enormous, with a total height of 74 feet and 43 feet in diameter, but instead of the globular shape used in the earlier balloons, this had a decidedly strange appearance, with according to a contemporary account, a pyramidal top, a prismatic central section and a truncated cone at the bottom. It was constructed from two layers of paper, with a layer of linen in between for reinforcement. It was supposed to be demonstrated before members of the royal family at Versailles, but the Montgolfiers decided to have a trial run with an ascent from Réveillon's garden, before an invited audience that included members of the Academie. The last thing they wanted was a fiasco in front of royalty. Because of its size, the balloon was brought in sections to the garden, where they were stitched together. On 11 September everything was ready for the trail flight.

At first, everything went well. A special stage was erected in the garden, with a central hole to which the neck of the balloon could be fitted and a furnace underneath to heat the air. It was held in position by a frame and ropes and twenty men were kept busy, ensuring that there were no folds that could cause cracks as the envelope expanded. The fire of wool and straw was lit, and any of the spectators who had also been present at the Charles experiment must have been impressed by the speed with which the balloon filled compared with the laborious process of inflating the hydrogen balloon. In a mere ten minutes the balloon had risen high above the heads of the crowd. It lifted a short distance from its moorings, but it required considerable force to keep it from breaking free. It was, it seemed, a great triumph; but within minutes triumph turned to disaster. A violent storm broke out with high winds and lashing rain. The handlers made valiant efforts to bring the balloon down to safety, but the rain made it sodden and unwieldy and the wind began to tear it to shreds. The balloon that was to have been the glory of Versailles was a total wreck.

The Montgolfiers now had a difficult choice: to have the humiliating task of informing the king that the flight expected to take place in just a week's time was cancelled, or use the next seven days to make a brand new balloon. They bravely opted for the latter course.

No one has ever given a satisfactory explanation of why the ruined balloon was built to such an odd shape: L.T.C. Rolt in his book *The Aeronauts* suggested that it might have been intended to look like a flying royal pavilion. In any case, there was now no time left for such niceties, and they opted for a conventional slightly pear-shaped balloon, at a more modest height of 57 feet and 41 feet in diameter. There was time to make it suitably resplendent as fitted a royal occasion, with brilliant blue and gold decoration. In just four days it was ready, given a short, tethered test flight and then taken to Versailles on the appointed day.

The Montgolfiers were able to complete their arrangements for the launch behind a screen, which must have added to the general sense of excitement. For most of those present, this would have been the very first balloon flight they had ever witnessed. Joseph and Etienne were treated to a royal banquet before the great event, after which the crowd of courtiers gathered to wait for King Louis and Marie Antoinette. The royal couple made a brief inspection of the balloon at close quarters, but were probably deterred from stopping too long by the stench of the furnace; burning wool is not a pleasant aroma.

The Montgolfiers had suggested that this might be the occasion for the first flight by a human being, but the king vetoed the idea on the grounds that it was too dangerous. Instead a wickerwork basket was slung under the balloon and the honour of being the first living creatures to make a balloon flight, though they probably did not appreciate the honour, went to a sheep, a duck and a cockerel.

So, on 19 September 1783, all was ready for this momentous experiment. Astronomers were placed at strategic high points on the palace to measure the height to which it rose – and as a check a barometer was added to the basket along with the livestock. When all was ready, three cannon were fired, and as the noise of the third reverberated around the palace grounds, the balloon rose into the air to tremendous applause. It drifted off on a light breeze, and some enthusiasts tried to follow it on foot. It was soon spotted slowly dropping down into the Vaucrasson forest, just about three kilometres from Versailles. Joseph had predicted a much longer flight, but no one felt in any way less than enthralled by the spectacle. Even the unwilling passengers survived: the basket was badly damaged, but when the followers reached the site, they found the sheep was placidly nibbling the grass, the duck was wandering around and only the cockerel seemed to have damaged one wing, but it turned out he'd been kicked by the sheep. The sight was an inspiration to a young scientist, who was among the first to arrive on the scene, His name was Jean-François Pilâtre de Rozier. He became an instant enthusiast and was to play an important role in the next stage of development. Human beings were about to take to the air.

CHAPTER TWO

Manned Flight

In spite of the successful flight by the sheep, duck and cock, there still existed considerable doubts about the advisability and safety of allowing human beings to go up in a balloon. The nature of earth's atmosphere was only dimly understood and there was a general theory among scientists that it wrapped the earth in a layer that was the same thickness no matter where you stood; whether you were down in a low valley or at the top of the highest mountain, there would still be exactly the same depth of air above your head. In other words, the atmosphere undulated, following the contours of the land. So, although Europe's highest mountain, Mont Blanc, rose to 4807 metres, no one believed that the atmosphere at the summit bore any resemblance to the atmosphere reached by a balloon starting down at sea level and climbing to the same height. This did not deter the Montgolfiers from planning a manned flight, but to do so they needed royal approval and the king was not inclined

Pilâtre de Rozier had the honour of being the first aeronaut to ascend by balloon.

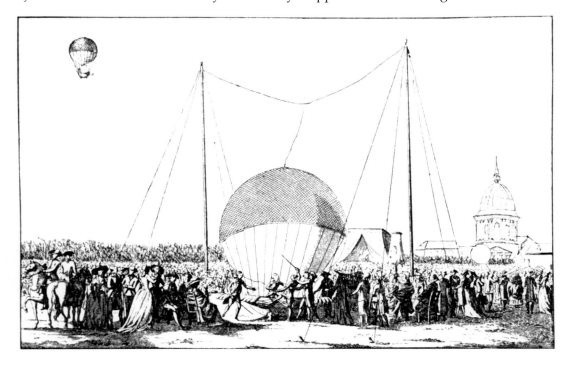

to agree to the experiment; his experts had convinced him that to go a great height in a balloon was a death sentence. The king did, however, come up with a solution to the dilemma. He agreed to a flight provided two criminals acted as the guinea pigs; they would be encouraged to volunteer by the promise that if, as was thought highly unlikely, they survived, they would be granted free pardons.

Pilâtre de Rozier, who had chased the earlier flight, was horrified: 'What! Have vile criminals received the glory of being the first to fly into the air? No, no, that will not do.' He was an interesting young man, born at Metz in 1754, where his father, an ex-soldier, kept an inn. As this was a garrison town, he prospered and young Jean-François became interested in studying the drugs in use at the military hospital and he decided that he should go to Paris to study chemistry and physics at the age of eighteen. He went on to teach the two subjects at the Academy in Reims, where he attracted the attention of the Comte de Provence, Louis XIV's brother. He was put in charge of the Comte's Cabinet of Natural History, and in due time he opened his own little museum, where he gave scientific lectures, and made a study of gases. His party piece was to inhale hydrogen, then blow it out and ignite it in a flash of flame.

So we have him determined to fly in a balloon, and also with the sort of aristocratic connections that were needed to overcome the king's resistance. He managed to persuade the Duchess of Polignac to take up his cause. She had come to Versailles in 1775 and had instantly become a great favourite of Marie Antoinette; he could hardly have found a better ambassador. They were joined in the venture by the Marquis d'Arlandes, an infantry officer in the French Royal Guard. He was also prepared to press the case for a manned flight, but only on one condition: he should travel with Pilâtre de Rozier and share the glory.

The Montgolfiers now had a heavy responsibility. It was one thing to risk the lives of a couple of birds and a sheep, quite another when the passengers were two men, both of whom were favourites at court. De Rozier, not surprisingly, took a personal interest in the construction of the new balloon. It is generally agreed that the fabric was slightly heavier and stronger than on earlier versions, but when it comes to the dimensions there is far less certainty, though the likeliest figures give a height of around 75 feet and a diameter of 45 feet, in English units, not French. The fire was contained in a wrought iron basket slung below the neck and attached by chains. Around this was a wickerwork gallery for the two aviators, with

The illustration
shows the
various pieces
of equipment
needed to produce
hydrogen and to
inflate a balloon.

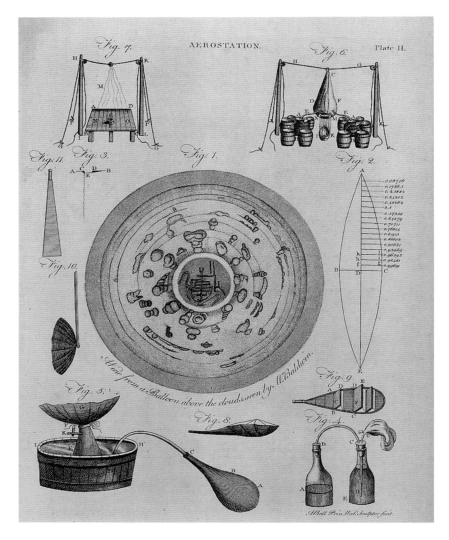

ports through which they could feed the fire. As with all the early balloons it was quite a gaudy affair, decorated in blue and gold with royal ciphers and signs of the zodiac.

Once again, the manufacture took place at the factory in Faubourg St Antoine, near enough to the centre of Paris to attract the interested and the merely curious. The crowds gathered round outside the factory and though the *Journal de Paris* declared rather snootily that nothing was happening that could possibly interest the hoi polloi, the numbers grew steadily. The crucial moment came on Wednesday 15 October 1783 when the fire was lit, the balloon inflated and de Rozier climbed into the gallery. The balloon was allowed to lift a few feet, while still firmly tethered, but the weight of the man made it seriously unstable, so it was brought down again and ballast added to the opposite side of the gallery to balance it again. It was now allowed to reach the full length of the tether, rising to a height of over 80 feet. The fire was kept stoked and de Rozier remained aloft for more than four minutes, before allowing the balloon to gently descend back to earth. As it neared the ground the excited balloonist jumped from the gallery, causing the balloon to tip dangerously; the golden rule of ballooning is to stay in the basket until everything is stable – even if you finish up stuck in an ungainly position with your legs in the air. Relieved of his weight the balloon shot skywards again, but fortunately the rope took the strain – otherwise it might have disappeared over the horizon and a search party would have had to set out to try and find it. As it was he was able to make a second ascent the same day. By now, a large crowd was beginning to gather outside the premises, hoping to see more flights. But the following day, there was a strong breeze blowing and it was decided it would be too dangerous to attempt any ascents.

Over the next few days there were more ascents and the tethering rope was lengthened to 300 feet. This gave the crowds ample opportunity to witness the event, and to see what might have been the first ballooning accident. A puff of wind blew the balloon sideways where it caught in the branches of a nearby tree. De Rozier simply added more straw to the fire to provide extra lift and it rose up with no damage done. On the third ascent on Sunday 19 October, the ballast was removed to make way for a passenger, Girond de Villette and they stayed aloft for nine minutes. After that it was finally the turn of the Marquis d'Arlande to take his place and enjoy his first ever flight – and to get ready to take his place when the balloon was finally set free.

This historic first manned free flight was scheduled for 20 November and the take off site was the grounds of the Château La Muette, home to the Dauphin in the Bois de Boulogne. The event was intended to be kept secret, only to be watched by the Dauphin himself and invited friends, but it was inevitable, given the excitement already caused by the tethered flight, that word would leak out, and as a result a large crowd thronged the area. But the day was ruined by stormy, wet weather that made a flight impossible. That did not deter the crowd from turning up the next day in the hope of seeing something. Given the seriousness of the occasion, the Montgolfiers were taking no chances; they organised yet one more tethered lift to ensure everything was in order. But once again, the unpredictable Parisian weather played its tricks on them; a sudden gust of wind caught the balloon and almost carried it away, and although the launch party managed to retrieve it safely, it had been quite badly damaged and there were several tears in the fabric. The cautious Montgolfiers had prepared for all contingencies, and soon seamstresses were at work mending the tears. In just two hours it was ready again.

By early afternoon, the sky had cleared, the wind had dropped and conditions were perfect for a launch. De Rozier and the Marquis climbed into the gallery and at 1.54 p.m. the balloon was released and rose gently into the sky and began drifting on a light breeze towards the Seine. The two men, on the opposite sides of the gallery waved enthusiastically to the cheering crowds below as they made their stately progress over the rooftops of Paris. The watchers had no means of knowing that on the balloon everything was not going quite as planned. The Marquis d'Arlandes wrote his own detailed account of the momentous flight.

Following the success of the Montgolfiers, hot air balloons were exhibited in many different countries. This colourful scene shows a fashionable crowd watching an ascent in Aranjuez, Spain.

At first it seems they were so preoccupied by the novel experience that they were scarcely aware of any movement, until they realised that La Muette was already out of sight and they were looking down on the confluence of the Oise and the Seine. The Marquis had to be constantly reminded to stop admiring the view and pay some attention to feeding the fire or they were in danger of getting a closer view of the river than they wanted. At one point, there was a loud cracking noise from the balloon, and for a moment he was sure it had burst, but it was simply a sudden air current that was speeding them on their way. Another loud crack suggested one of the cords had snapped, and when he inspected the fabric, he discovered a number of smouldering holes in the cloth, which he damped down with a sponge, but more alarmingly the bottom of the cloth was coming away from its supporting circle. Closer examination showed that only two cords were broken and there was no immediate danger, which was just as well as they were crossing Paris where finding a landing space would have been all but impossible. The Marquis was increasingly concerned about their position and was constantly urging de Rozier to land, but he held out until he could see a safe landing place. They headed for a gap between two mills and came down safely; the Marquis jumped out but Pilâtre finished up beneath the collapsed balloon. He emerged unscathed and the two pioneers were greeted by the Duc de Chartres, who had followed their progress on horseback. They had landed about five miles away from where they started, in the area of the Butte-aux-Cailles, in what is now the 13th arrondissement in the south east of Paris.

The somewhat laconic account left by the Marquis does not do justice to the very real danger they were in. Those little fires could have grown, the holes could have become bigger and the whole balloon would have collapsed. Even though the fabric remained more or less intact, it was still obvious that they needed to land as quickly as possible but finding somewhere to put down safely in a largely urban area was itself fraught with danger. Their predicament would have taxed the skill of any experienced balloonist, but not only had they no experience, but nor had anyone else who could have advised them before they set off on their pioneering flight. It did not, however, settle the big question of the day: did the future lie with the hot air or the hydrogen balloon?

Jacques Charles remained convinced that the hydrogen balloon was far superior to the hot air version and promptly set out to plan a manned flight of his own. The first prototype had been a very modest affair, and now something altogether grander was needed and in designing it Charles produced a particularly fine and manageable balloon. The new version was 27 ft 6in in diameter and constructed of carefully designed strips of rubberised silk, shaped like the outer skin of an orange segment. These were sewn together and the end result was an almost perfect sphere. The resemblance to a globe has led to the top and bottom of this and other balloons being known as the north and south poles. There were other changes; the troublesome stop cock at the south pole on the previous balloon was replaced by an open neck, which allowed the gas to escape as it expanded when the balloon ascended into the thinner upper atmosphere or became overheated. A valve that was kept closed by a spring was placed at the north pole, from which a rope hung down to the basket. By pulling on this cord, the valve could be opened and gas released, allowing the balloon to descend in a gentle, controlled fashion. The top half of the balloon was covered by netting to which a wooden ring was attached at the equator. The basket was then suspended from this ring. This was not altogether satisfactory, as the hoop tended to pinch in the centre of the balloon and chafe the fabric. The car itself was an oblong 8-foot by 4- foot and 3ft 6in deep. An oblong shape is far from ideal, as it is difficult to keep in balance. As with all the early balloons it was covered in highly decorated cloth, which together with the alternating red and yellow segments of the balloon itself, gave the whole affair a suitably gaudy appearance; this was, after all, at the tail end of that most extravagant of artistic style, the rococo.

The crew for the first planned flight of the new balloon consisted of Charles himself and Nicolas-Louis Robert, who was not only an intrepid aviator, ready to risk his neck in a pioneering venture, but an inventor in his own right. In later life he was to develop the very first machine for making continuous sheets of paper. The flight was planned for 1 December 1783 with an ascent from the Jardin des Tuileries. One of the ornamental lakes had been covered over to provide the launch site, but Charles had no doubt seen the near riots that occurred when the crowds came to watch the inflation of the Montgolfier balloon, so he decided to carry out the very slow process of inflating with hydrogen in a spot sheltered by trees in the Grande Avenue. It could then be brought to the site in front of the Palace des Tuileries. Contemporary accounts claim that 400,000 spectators turned up for the great event. If the figure is even remotely accurate that is about half the population of Paris, but as we know from our own time estimating crowd sizes is a tricky business. But it was certainly an immense number and gives a good idea of the excitement caused by this new enthralling activity of ballooning.

The car was attached to the balloon, which was held down by assistants and ballast added in the form of sandbags to balance out the lift and keep everything grounded until it was ready to be released. Charles and Robert had little idea what to expect once they rose into the sky, so they took many precautions – heavy clothing and blankets to keep themselves warm, ample provisions which included a considerable quantity of wine, a thermometer and a barometer to measure altitude. Charles had taken the added precaution of creating a tiny balloon that could be released to give him an indication of wind speed and direction at altitude. But instead of releasing it himself, he passed it to his great rival Joseph Montgolfier, a generous gesture that acknowledged his competitor's own great achievement. It rose sharply and drifted off to the north-east on a gentle air current. Conditions it seems were perfect and Charles and Robert stepped on board and threw out some of the ballast so that the balloon could lift. At 1.45 that afternoon a cannon was fired to signal all was ready, the balloon was released and soared into the sky.

Not surprisingly, given the relative densities of hydrogen and hot air it rose far faster than the Montgolfier and seems to have caught the crowd by surprise. There was a momentary hush, then Charles and Robert were seen waving flags to show all was well, and the cheers resounded round the city. The temperature was a comfortable 12°C so it was decided to jettison the blankets and heavy clothing: the first blanket finished up draped across the dome of a church, neatly wrapping it up, rather like a prototype of the work of the artist Christo, who later wrapped the Pont Neuf. They floated on across the outskirts of Paris, crossing the Seine twice, where it makes a great u-bend near St.Denis and continued their stately progress northward at a height of almost 1000 feet. Their progress was smooth and steady, and excited spectators shouted encouragement from the ground, while the two balloonists waved their flags and shouted back 'Long live the King'. Once clear of Paris they found themselves drifting across an empty plain and decided it was time to come down and they made a very controlled approach. But as they got closer to the ground, they found themselves heading towards a large tree. Charles simply threw out one of the ballast bags to allow them to rise above the topmost branches and then calmly continued their descent to a perfect landing.

They had covered a distance of 31 miles from their take off in the Tuileries and as they descended local people rushed out to follow their progress. They had arrived near the hamlet of Nesle – not to be confused with the larger town of Nesle in the Pas de Calais. As well as the local people who helped ground the balloon, they were soon joined by a group from Paris who had followed their progress on horseback: the Duc de Chartres, the Duc de Fitz-James and an English enthusiast called Farrer, who rushed to embrace Charles. But Charles was not ready to accept lengthy congratulations; there was still hydrogen in the balloon, though it was partly deflated and he was keen to go up yet again, this time in a solo flight. With one less passenger, the balloon shot skywards, and the barometer showed that he had reached an altitude of around 10,000 feet. Where he had previously enjoyed a warm almost spring-like sunshine before, now with the added height and the sun sinking below the horizon, it was becoming quite cold. He developed a sharp pain in one ear, possibly due to the sudden change in pressure and decided it was time to come down. Once again, the descent was beautifully controlled; throwing out ballast when it started to get uncomfortably rapid and he made a perfect landing near the woods of Tour de Lay.

The whole day had been a triumph, but Charles never flew again. Perhaps the solo flight had turned out to be a little too alarming, or possibly he had set out to prove a point, that the hydrogen balloon was as viable as, and arguably superior to, the hot air balloon. He had done so and felt no need to take matters any further. It had not actually settled the debate over which was the better solution for flying, hot air or hydrogen, but it was the Charles balloon that caught the public imagination and led to a craze for miniature balloons, mostly based on the spherical Charles design.

The Montgolfiers had certainly not quitted the field, and planned the largest balloon yet constructed, over 130 feet high and just over 100 feet in diameter. It was built in a suburb of Lyon and named *Le Fleselle* after the governor of Lyon, M. le Fleselle. Having achieved human flight the Montgolfiers thought they might try something a little more ambitious and proposed sending a horse up, a proposal that seems hopelessly impractical. One only has to imagine the terrifying effect on a horse suddenly shooting up to the sky to know how violently it would react. It was de Rozier who persuaded them that another human flight in a conventional wicker basket was more sensible.

The flight was beset with problems, largely caused by the bad wintry weather, which caused some damage that had to be repaired. After many mishaps, the huge affair was finally inflated and during the test it took the combined strength of fifty burly men to hold it down. This was by far the most ambitious flight, and this time the fire basket was to be fed with wood as well as straw and it was planned to take six people. De Rozier as the only one who had previously piloted a balloon had to go and Joseph Montgolfier also decided to take a trip. Various members of the French aristocracy vied for the remaining four places, which went to Prince Charles de Ligne and three Counts. The launch date was set for 19 January, but when it came to the great day, de Rozier felt they had overestimated the load that could be safely carried, and one of the aristocrats would have to remain behind. They were having none of it and accounts of what happened next are a little varied. All agree that the four men jumped into the basket, at which point they drew either swords or pistols and defied anyone to remove them. There was no arguing with them and de Rozier had no option but to let them remain, and as the monstrous balloon was released one of the helpers jumped in as well.

It rose to a height of 3,000 feet. The earlier mishaps that had caused the damage to the fabric had been repaired but, as it soon turned out, not very successfully. A large tear appeared, allowing the hot air to escape faster than it could be replenished even by feverishly stoking up the fire. The balloon that had shot skywards now began a slow descent, gradually deflating. Only three minutes after it had lifted off the vast balloon was back on the ground, with its passengers unharmed. It had not been the most successful of flights, but even so the huge crowd was thrilled and the short flight did nothing to stem the enthusiasm for this new and exciting pastime of ballooning. Now the excitement spread outside the French borders for the very first time, and many more people were to take to the air in different parts of Europe.

CHAPTER THREE

Balloon Mania

The initial successes by the Montgofiers and Charles led to a great wave of enthusiasm for all things connected with ballooning in France. Baron Grimm wrote: 'Among all our circle of friends, at all our meals, in the antechambers of our lovely women, as in our academic schools, all one hears is talk of experiments, atmospheric air, inflammable air, flying cars, journeys in the sky.' Balloon motifs adorned everything from ladies garments to teapots and Benjamin Franklin, who was in Paris at the time, described small balloons as being on sale everywhere. He was invited out to 'tea and balloon' and to a fete organised by the duc de Chartres, in which these little balloons were handed out to guests. He bought several himself and emptied the hydrogen from one and sent it to his friend Richard Price in England – probably the first hydrogen balloon to be seen in Britain. But not everyone was satisfied with having balloons as mere unusual toys and others were willing to try this new and exciting pastime of taking to the air.

In Italy the Chevalier Paul Andreani arranged for a hot air balloon to be built to his own design, in which the brazier was attached to a hoop, suspended by lines from the balloon, and instead of a surrounding gallery had a basketwork car suspended beneath it. Quite what they would have done had the fire got out of control it is difficult to imagine, but in the event, he took off on 25 February 1784, was airborne for twenty minutes and completed the first ascent to take place outside France. That May saw the first ascent by women. They were four ladies: a marchioness: two countesses and a solitary commoner entitled simply Mlle de Lagarde. Their flight, however, remained tethered to the ground.

The honour of being the first woman to fly free went to Élisabeth Thible. Not a great deal is known about her, though she is generally referred to as having been an opera singer and to have been married at one time. The balloon was to be piloted by Monsieur Fleurant with the Count Jean Baptiste de Laurencin, but the count had his first experience in the near disastrous flight of the giant Montgolfière and declined the invitation. Mme Thible was invited to take his place and did so with a great deal of panache. The flight took place on 4 June 1784 in a balloon named La Gustave in honour of King Gustav III, who was present for the occasion. Mme Thible arrived dressed as the Roman Goddess Minerva, but also sporting a large, feathered hat, which she must have thought rather more fetching than the metal helmet the goddess is usually depicted as wearing. She certainly showed no sign of fear and not only helped stoke the fire but found time to sing a couple of duets with Fleurant from Monsigny's opera *La Belle Arsene*. The flight went well, but there was an awkward landing and Mme Thible suffered a sprained ankle - a small price to play for earning herself a place in aviation history. She was only the first of a number of intrepid female balloonists, some of whom we shall be meeting shortly.

The arguments still continued as to which was the better form of balloon – hydrogen or hot air. The Montgolfière had the advantage of being easier to inflate but it suffered from a serious problem – it was all too prone to catch fire. Landing was especially dangerous and the fire basket had to be jettisoned before the balloon touched down to avoid everything going up in flames. Even with this precaution, the hot air balloons suffered several fiery endings. Flights continued but were generally comparatively short and

An artist's impression of Count Zambecarri's rescue from his balloon's descent into the Adriatic.

it was rare for a balloon to be reusable after its initial flight. The hydrogen balloon began to gain in popularity as the hydrogen generation system was steadily improved and because the skin could be made out of more robust material, re-use was not a problem. Its superiority was confirmed on 19 September 1784 when Cadet Robert set off with M. Collin-Hullin in an unusual hydrogen balloon. It was elongated, looking rather like a very fat sausage, and the basket had oars that were intended to make it steerable. It is very doubtful if the latter had any real value, but it was a remarkable flight. Taking off from Paris at midday it travelled north and ended up 186 km away at Beuvry not far from the French coast. By a strange coincidence the Prince de Ghistelles was holding a fete for his tenants at his chateau, where the highlight was going to be the release of a small hot air balloon. Instead the spectators were to enjoy the far more exciting spectacle of a manned hydrogen balloon dropping down in the grounds. An engraving in Gaston Tissondier's *Histoire des Ballons* shows the landing with, close to the chateau, a windmill which the aeronauts only just avoided hitting.

In Britain, the whole affair was more than a little embarrassing for the learned gentlemen of the Royal Society, the country's most prestigious body of scientists, who had declared the whole thing impossible. However, there was another society of men interested in the latest developments in science and industry, the Lunar Society of Birmingham – so called because they arranged to meet on nights when there was a full moon to light their way home. It included among its members such famous men as the pioneers of steam, Matthew Boulton and James Watt, the potter Josiah Wedgwood and the polymath Dr Erasmus Darwin. The latter loved anything that smacked of novelty in the sciences. In January 1784 he made Britain's first hydrogen balloon and decided to use it to send a letter to his fellow members of the Society who met at Boulton's Soho House. Things did not quite go to plan, as he himself explained in a letter: 'You heard we sent your society an air-balloon which was calculated to have fallen in your garden at Soho. But the wicked wind carried it to Sir Edward Littleton.' It was the first letter ever to be sent by airmail – even if it never reached its destination. The description of it as being an air-balloon is misleading – at that time hydrogen was often referred to as inflammable air.

Darwin's balloon encouraged Boulton to experiment with this intriguing form of flight. Later in 1784, he was in Cornwall with Watt on one of their regular visits to the county that was the most

important purchasers of their steam engines for draining the tin and copper mines. Boulton constructed a paper balloon, which he coated with varnish and then inflated using a mixture of hydrogen and air. He tied a firecracker to the bottom of the balloon, lit it and sent it soaring skywards. The balloon was a mile away before the cracker went off and the balloon exploded with a satisfactorily loud bang. Everyone cheered and declared themselves delighted with the experiment, apart from the rather dour Watt who complained of being very disappointed, for he had hoped to use the flight as an experiment to investigate the noise made by thunder, and he couldn't hear properly because of all the cheering.

Darwin and Boulton were not the only ones to experiment with balloons in Britain, but they could claim to be the first British subjects to make the experiment. The honour of being the first true pioneer of ballooning in the country went to an Italian Count Francesco Zambeccari, a colourful character born in Bologna in 1752. After studying in Parma, he left for Spain where he first joined the Guardia Real, the Royal Guard and then the Spanish navy, where he saw action. It is not certain quite what he had done wrong, but we do know that he fell foul of the Inquisition and made a hurried departure. His first stop was Paris where he was just in time to see the Montgolfiers' first unmanned flight. He was very impressed, and when he reached London he joined forces with another Italian, Michael Biaganni, who had a business making artificial flowers from silk at his premises in Cheapside. Together they manufactured a modest 5ft diameter gas balloon, which they flew from the Cheapside site and which was eventually found in Waltham Abbey. Encouraged by their success, they decided to make a second, bigger balloon and make some money from the enterprise. This was twice as large and tickets were sold for the launch from the grounds of the Honourable Artillery Company. This flight was a respectable 40 miles, ending up at the village of Graffham on the South Downs. The farmer who found it was the second to make a profit from the enterprise – he exhibited it in the village hall and charged one penny admission.

Zambeccari went on to collaborate with Vincent Lombardi, whose career we shall be looking at shortly, but he was a restless man and was soon off on his travels again, this time to St. Petersburg to join the Russian navy. Eventually he returned to Italy, married and returned to ballooning. This time he went in for manned flights, but not always with the greatest success. In 1803, he and a companion, Dr Andreoli, set off on a flight which was intended to be used for various scientific experiments. All went well at first and they came down to land near Capo d'Argine. Zambeccari anchored the balloon to a tree, but in doing so the car tipped, spilling 'spirits of wine' that

caught fire. There was a larger container of the spirits and soon that was ablaze as well, with the fire catching the aeronaut's clothes and threatening the net and ropes of the balloon. While the Count was dowsing the flames with water, Andreoli made his escape, shinning down the anchor rope and dropping to the ground. Without his extra weight the balloon rose rapidly, with the Count still on board fighting the flames. What happened next is told in an account from the Philosophical Magazine of 1804, using the Count's own description of the event.

Lunardi's flight from the Royal Artillery grounds.

'The balloon was then carried by a strong current of air towards the Adriatic and at 3 o'clock the Count perceived the coast of Comachio, but from such an elevation that he could hardly distinguish it. Soon after he fell into the sea at about the distance of 25 Italian miles from the coast. The car, which was half burnt sunk, and Count Zambecarri was held fast by the ropes of the balloon, had the water often up to his neck. Apprehensive that lassitude would oblige him to let go his hold, or that he should be overcome by sleep he endeavoured to fasten himself to a rope. By means of a bit of glass he detached one from the balloon, and fastened it round his body, the other end of it being fixed to the machine. In this situation he floated on the water for some hours, the balloon being still inflated.

'At length about six in the evening, he observed seven fishing-boats, the people in four of which being struck with terror betook themselves to flight, imagining that they saw some strange kind of sea monster. The other three approached and took from the water the unfortunate aeronaut half burnt having spent four hours at sea amidst the most dreadful anguish.'

The Count was to have another forced landing in the Adriatic, but this did nothing to deter him from experimenting with balloons and making more flights. His last took place in September 1812, when once again his balloon caught fire. This time, however, he was unable to quench the flames and the brave aeronaut was killed.

All these early pioneers were acting in an atmosphere of great uncertainty as to whether the whole thing was a serious experiment in aviation or little more than an amusing toy. The *Morning Herald*, a newspaper founded in 1780, suggested that everyone should 'laugh this new folly out of practice as soon as possible'. This did not prevent several people from attempting to make and fly balloons, though it is difficult today to decide which accounts were real and which fabricated. One story tells of 'an old Jew' being carried aloft to a height of over 300 feet before descending again unharmed to the acclaim of a large crowd. Somehow one has a mental image of a solemn rabbinical gentleman gently rising into the sky and just as gently drifting down again; one would like it to be true, but it probably isn't.

The story of James Tytler, however, is well authenticated and he is probably the most extraordinary character in this whole story of balloon pioneers. He was born in Forfarshire in Scotland, where his father was a Presbyterian minister, who taught him theology and the classics, possibly with the hope that he would follow his footsteps and enter the clergy. Instead Tytler went to Edinburgh University where he studied medicine. He was then apprenticed for a year to a ship's doctor and although there is no record of his graduation, he later attached the initials MA to his name. On returning to Scotland he set up in business as a pharmacist but went bankrupt and was forced to depart for England to escape his many debtors. He started up a second pharmacy business, married and was eventually to father five children, though he and his wife later separated. His new venture was no more successful than the first, so he found a new occupation. He returned to Scotland and began to earn a living as a writer. He had earlier produced a number of religious pamphlets, but his most successful book was very different: *Ranger's Impartial List of the Ladies of Pleasure of Edinburgh* - a title that might give a clue as to why he and his wife went their separate ways. After that he became editor of the 2nd edition of the Encyclopaedia Britannica. He worked on the publication from 1777-84 and not only acted as editor but also wrote a great many of the entries, and he was also to contribute a great deal to the third edition.

Quite how he became interested in ballooning is something of a mystery but he decided to develop a balloon with an Edinburgh chemist called Scott. Probably he saw it as an opportunity to make some money; people would, he thought, pay to see what would be the very first manned balloon flight in Britain. He and Scott experimented with a small hydrogen balloon, which travelled for some twenty miles, but when it came to his own flight he opted for a Montgolfière. Its shape was unlike any other balloon that had been built so far – 40ft high and 30ft in diameter. It had a massive furnace, which weighed about 300 pounds. The idea was to present the grand spectacle of Tytler rising serenely above the city of Edinburgh. In the event, everything that could go wrong, did go wrong. On 7 August 1784, Tytler began to inflate the balloon, but it caught fire, the chains holding the grate broke and the gallery was damaged. It was repaired and a second attempt was made the next day. This time all seemed to be in order, when a sudden violent gust of wind caught the balloon which, according to Tyler, tipped it over, allowing the hot air to spill out. To appease the crowd, Tytler decided that the only solution was to get as much hot air into the balloon as possible, get rid of both the furnace and the gallery and suspend himself beneath the fabric – 'like a log' as he wrote later. In this manner he made two short flights on 25 August and 1 September. They were not glorious flights – mere leaps as Tytler put it – but it did earn him the honour of being the first British aeronaut.

Tytler was to make two further attempts to make the grand flight he had dreamed of, but both ended disastrously. The first came to an abrupt end with the balloon escaping and crashing into a tree; the second was simply a fiasco. It leaked so badly that it remained rooted to the ground. The disconsolate Tytler was widely ridiculed by commentators who themselves had no notion of the problems involved in ballooning and would certainly not have been prepared to risk their lives in the enterprise. He left Scotland forever, going first to Ireland, then America where he died. It had been an eventful life – as well as the various occupations already mentioned, he had written songs, poetry and political pamphlets, in one of which he had denounced the House of Commons as 'a vile junto of aristocrats' – an article that resulted in his being charged with sedition and hastened his departure from Scotland. Today he is chiefly remembered for his contribution to the development of the famous encyclopaedia rather than for his exploits as a balloonist. He was never to achieve the fame that came to our next aeronaut.

Vincenzo Lunardi was to achieve the renown and public acclaim that had so sadly eluded Tytler. He started with considerable social advantages. He was born into an aristocratic Neapolitan family and travelled for some years in France before entering the diplomatic service. It has to be said that there is some debate about the facts of his early life – he was much given to self-aggrandisement. He arrived in England as part of the entourage of the Neapolitan Ambassador, Prince Caramanico. Once settled in the country he anglicised his first name to Vincent.

In 1784 he declared his intention to make a flight and appealed for subscriptions to cover the costs of making a hydrogen balloon. Subscribers would be able to visit the Lyceum in The Strand, where it was to be constructed and would have admission to the enclosure to watch the actual ascent. In spite of earlier doubts about ballooning by eminent scientists, it was Sir Joseph Banks, the famous botanist and President of the Royal Society, who opened the subscription list, lending the enterprise a seal of approval. Lunardi had reached an agreement that the flight should take place from the grounds of the Chelsea Hospital and in return the pensioners who lived there would benefit from a share of the profits. The money, however, was a little slow to materialise and in the meantime two potential rivals appeared on the scene. The first was an extraordinary balloon in the shape of a Chinese temple. This fantastic device was the work of the Chevalier de Moret, a self-proclaimed genius. As ever the crowd paid to see the spectacle, but there was never any possibility that this ludicrous contraption would ever get off the ground. It took a while for this to sink in, but when it became obvious to everyone in the crowd there was a stampede to destroy the monstrosity while the Chevalier made his escape – with, of course, the proceeds. The second attempt was a more genuine affair and the work of Dr John Sheldon, a distinguished surgeon and Professor of Anatomy at the Royal College. His aim was to use the flight for scientific research, but there was only one short ascent, with the balloon tethered and at a second attempt it caught fire and was completely destroyed. Sheldon abandoned the enterprise. The way was open for Lunardi – or at least it seemed to be.

The two fiascos had one unfortunate effect. They appear to have convinced the authorities at Chelsea Hospital that it would be folly to allow a similar event on their property and withdrew their permission. Lunardi was a volatile character. When anything went wrong, he was immediately filled with the deepest despair, convinced that catastrophe was inevitable, and told all his friends how he felt – 'I am now sunk into the utmost depth of distress'. He then promptly got down to remedying the situation and on this occasion, he was quickly able to find a new venue. The site was to be the Honourable Artillery Company's training ground at Moorfields in the City of London, the site now known as Artillery Gardens. Lunardi now had a partner in his plans, George Biggins who was an eminent amateur scientist, Fellow of the Royal Society and inventor of the percolator coffee pot. There is no doubt that his scientific background must have been hugely important in designing the balloon, which had several distinctive features. This was a hydrogen balloon and conventionally globular: the shape that had become standard. One feature the Lunardi balloon lacked was a valve at the north pole, which meant that there was no means of releasing gas. It was not clearly understood that as a balloon went higher air pressure would reduce and that this would inevitably result in the gas expanding. It did, however have a very good arrangement for the passengers, with a simple, plain wickerwork basket suspended from a hoop below the balloon – no fanciful gondolas and pavilions here.

The day of the ascent was 15 September 1784. The task of filling the balloon was entrusted to Doctor George Fordyce a medical doctor with an interest in chemistry. He had devised a special mechanism, in which dilute sulphuric acid was dripped down into a mixture of zinc and iron fillings. The gas was then passed through a weak alkaline solution to neutralise any acid fumes and prevent damage to the balloon fabric. It was a reasonable idea in theory. Manufacturing the hydrogen began the day before the ascent but was painfully slow. Dr Fordyce decided to retire for the night and leave it to his crew to continue the work – but it was apparently a chilly night and there's nothing like a drop of the hard stuff to warm the heart. When the doctor arrived the next day, the gang were in a drunken stupor and the apparatus unused. Fortunately, the Swiss inventor Pierre Aimé Argand, who had designed a new, improved oil lamp, turned up at the scene and offered his expertise, which was accepted. It was just as well as Argand noted that Dr Fordyce and Lunardi appeared to 'know little'.

Things did speed up, but a lot of time had been lost and by now a crowd estimated at 200,000 had assembled and were getting impatient. This was a hugely important occasion for Lunardi for there were some very august visitors, including the Prince of Wales. As the launch time passed and the balloon was still not fully inflated, the would-be aeronaut took a brave decision. He thought it unlikely there was enough gas in the balloon to carry two, but he was happy to make a solo ascent. He stepped into the car with his only travelling companions, a cat, a dog, a caged pigeon, a cold chicken and a good supply of wine. As he gave the sign for the crew to let go and he soared into the sky, the Prince of Wales raised his hat in salute and the rest of the crowd followed suit, many believing they would never see him again. Among the doubters was the king, who was watching Lunardi's progress through a telescope.

Meanwhile the airborne Lunardi was floating merrily over north London heading out into the Hertfordshire countryside. He was having a great time, quaffing wine – he eventually threw out an empty bottle – and enjoying the sensation of flying. His pet cat, however, was less happy and was apparently airsick. He decided it was time to touch down and put the unhappy animal out of its misery. He had brought oars along in the mistaken belief that he could row himself to ground. It is not clear exactly how he managed to land, but he did, handed the cat over for safe keeping, threw out some ballast and shot skywards again.

When it came time to bring the adventure to a close, he threw out a rope and shouted to some harvesters to grab it and hold in while he descended – but they simply declared the whole thing the work of the devil and bolted. It was a young woman, working in a nearby brew house, who heard Lunardi's shout and grabbed the line. The flight was over, with the landing in a field at Standon near Ware. The spot was marked by an engraved stone with a message that has all the hallmarks of Lunardi's own personality.

'Let Posterity know and knowing be astonished! That On the 15th day of September, 1784 Vincent Lunardi of Lucca in Tuscany the First Aerial Traveller in Britain mounting for the Artillery Ground in London and traversing the Regions of the Air for two Hours and fifteen Minutes in this Spot revisited the earth. On this Rude monument For Ages he recorded that wondrous enterprize successfully achieved by the powers of Chymestry and the fortitude of bloke That improvement in Science Which The Great Author of all Knowledge patronising by His Providence the Inventions of Mankind hath generously permitted to their benefit and his own Eternal Glory.'

The following year Lunardi planned another flight, this time with Biggins and an actress, Letitia Ann Sage. Not a great deal is known about the lady, who was originally one of three Hoare sisters, but took the name 'Sage' when she became the common law wife of a London haberdasher of that name. The basket was swathed with drapery, but Lunardi must have received something of a shock when the lady herself appeared. She wore a low-cut gown, which was perhaps not entirely appropriate for flying, but rather more startlingly she was not the sylph like figure he had expected. The lady, in her own account of the flight, cheerfully admitted to tipping the scales at over 200 pounds. There is a well-known illustration of the trio setting off in fine style, but it was produced before the event. For when it came to the take-off, the basket remained stubbornly grounded; there was simply too much weight. In some accounts, a Colonel Hastings had also been intending to take the trip. If he was present he was forced, like Lunardi himself, to step out of the basket and leave it to Biggins and Mrs Sage.

Inevitably, an exotic actress and a young man sailing above London and the countryside gave rise to scandal. We know they enjoyed a picnic of cold chicken and wine – cheerfully throwing out the empties – but there were suggestions that rather more went on while they were aloft. It has to be said there is absolutely no evidence to support the notion and she herself always denied it. What is known is that they eventually came down in a field of crops near Harrow. In the lady's own words, the farmer soon appeared and was 'abusive and savage to a degree' Accounts differ about what happened next, but in most stories she was slightly injured in the descent and was rescued by a group of boys from Harrow School, who had a whip round to pacify the farmer and carried the lady to the nearest pub to recover. One version has it there was just one boy – if so, he must have been a very strong lad! What all do agree is that the celebrations in the pub went on for a long time. So the first ascent by a woman in Britain came to an end and Mrs Sage did very well from the venture – writing her own account that became a popular best seller. She deserved her success and her day of glory. One has to remember that at this time ballooning was still a real novelty. The only man among those gathered at the start who had ever flown a balloon was Lunardi and he had stepped aside to allow the flight to get off the ground. Any balloon trip is something of an adventure, but to take one's first flight with a pilot who had also never flown before shows a degree of courage and sang froid.

Lunardi now took his balloon and all its essential equipment on a tour round Britain, starting in Liverpool, where he made two ascents. Large crowds gathered to see the spectacle and assumed that it was perfectly acceptable to demand a show – no matter what the weather conditions. On the second ascent there was a strong west to north west wind blowing ad even some voices in the crowd were raised calling out that it was too dangerous. By this time, however, Lunardi had acquired a nickname that proved to have excellent publicity value – the 'Daredevil Aeronaut'. Daredevils do not flinch at danger, so he insisted on flying. The balloon shot skywards and hurtled away on the strong wind. He eventually landed near the hamlet of Tarporley, roughly half way between Chester and Crewe. He threw out his anchor but the wind was too strong and the balloon simply kept going, almost bouncing over the ground, ripping through hedges and knocking a chimney off a cottage before it finally came to rest. It must have been an unnerving experience to say the least and the consequences could have been far worse, but it did nothing to deter Lunardi. His next stop would be Scotland.

As with all his projects, setbacks were treated as calamities – small successes triumphs – and there was no shortage of self-aggrandisement. The first problem came when the launch apparatus failed to arrive in Edinburgh from Liverpool. He had reached an agreement with a carter who had promised him the journey would take 16 days. The expected delivery day arrived but no equipment. The aeronaut immediately imagined all kinds of mishaps but was assured by the locals that it was highly unlikely that a lumbering cart would ever have been able to make the 220 mile journey in such a short time - and in due time his apparatus appeared. The next vexation soon arrived. For Lunardi it was essential that the whole event be undertaken with appropriate pomp and ceremony: a flag must be unfurled and cannon fired. But the authorities seemed disinclined to help and Lunardi at once began to think of abandoning the whole project – but it proved comparatively simple to iron out this difficulty and Lunardi's good humour was at once restored. He was able once again to dream of glory – and in particular to imagine the effect his ascent would have on the many beautiful Scots ladies who would be attending.

'Ah! What glory to ascend my AERIAL CHARIOT in their view! To be the object of *their* admiration! To have all their eyes turned towards me! All their prayers and wishes breathed forth for my safety! And to hear their wild acclamations!'

On 5 October 1785 Lunardi climbed into the gallery below his green, pink and yellow hydrogen balloon before a huge crowd in the grounds of George Heriot's School and in a charming gesture requested the Scots pioneer James Tytler to release the small test balloon that would indicate wind direction. It was blowing from the south so Lunardi equipped himself with a cork jacket as his route would be over the open waters of the Firth of Forth. But for the take-off he wore his usual colourful uniform.

Once airborne and over the water he was full of confidence. Seeing a boat below him, he swooped down to call out to the crew. 'I bid them *goodbye* and told them that it was in vain attempting to keep up with me! Then throwing out a bag of sand, I immediately ascended.' It was then that he discovered a vital fact about the atmosphere – the winds do not necessarily blow the same way at every altitude. Now instead of heading for the comfort of land, he appeared to be moving out to sea. He hastily put on his cork jacket and began adjusting his altitude until he was once again heading for the shore, or so he hoped, for he was now travelling above the clouds. But there were no more alarms and soon he was able to make a comfortable landing near the little weaving village of Ceres in Fife.

'I proceeded to CUPAR where I was received with JOY barely *inexpressible*! The *lower ranks* of *people* looked on me as a kind of Superior being: and I am in the inevitable strain of delicate flattery who says in my ear that LUNARD's arrival in this country will be celebrated for many years to come!'

Not all Lunardi's flights were so successful. In a flight from Glasgow, a local character called Lothian Tam got entangled with the ropes at take-off and was carried aloft. It was estimated that the balloon had reached a height of some six metres before anyone could cut him free. He fell to the ground but suffered no very serious injuries. The next flight from Edinburgh in December 1785 could have ended in total disaster, when he came down in the sea. A clergyman, Rev John Mill, showed little enthusiasm for Lunardi's earlier success and less sympathy for his later plight.

'A French man called Lunardi flew over the Firth of Forth in a Balloon, and lighted in Ceres parish, not far from Cupar, in Fife; and O! how much are the thoughtless multitude set on these and like foolish vanities to the neglect of the one thing needful. Afterwards, 'tis said when soaring upwards in the foresaid machine, he was driven by the wind down the Firth of Forth, and tumbled down into the sea near little Isle of May, where he had perished had not a boat been near who saved him and his machine.'

There were few more scathing on the subject of frivolities than Presbyterian ministers. But Lunardi was still enjoying the happy glow of adulation for his exploits; all that was to change with an attempted flight from Newcastle the following year. During the preparations some of the acid that was used to generate the hydrogen was spilled and the crew holding down the balloon ran off in a panic allowing it to rise. One of them, however, was caught up in the ropes and carried away. Eventually he fell and died of his injuries. The accident received wide and usually hostile comment, not least because the tragic victim was the son of the respected under-sheriff of Northumberland, Mr Heron. Although the accident was in no way his fault, Lunardi changed overnight from hero to villain. He left Britain and returned to Italy, where he continued to make several flights, including one which must have been very exciting beside Mount Vesuvius. He remained the daredevil throughout his notable flying career.

The contrast between Lunardi's early career could hardly have been more marked. At first, he was the darling of the crowds and so well known that he even made it into the world of fashion. Young ladies wore huge balloon-shaped bonnets known as Lunardis that became so popular that it was mentioned in one of Robert Burns' poems – *To a Louse.* He berates the creature saying it's all very well to take up residence on an old lady's head:

'But Miss's fine Lunardi, Fye!
How dare ye do't?'

But after the tragedy of Heron's death, he became an object of ridicule:

'Behold our Hero, comely, tall and fair,
His only food phlogisticated air,
Now on the wings of Mighty Winds he rides,
Now torn through Hedges, Duck's in Ocean's Tides;
Now drooping roams about from Town to Town
Collecting pennies t'inflate his poor balloon:
Pity the Wight and something to him give
To purchase gas to keep his frame alive.'

The reference to phlogisticated air is a reminder that although ballooning depended on the physical and chemical characteristics of gases, their nature was not clearly understood: it was still believed that when a substance burned it gave off a mysterious substance called phlogiston.

Although the first flights in Britain had been carried out by Italians, it was not long after Lunardi's pioneering venture that the first Englishman took to the skies. James Sadler came from a notably less flamboyant background: his parents were pastry cooks in Oxford, and he had followed them into the family business. He was, however, a young man blessed with scientific curiosity. For his first flight he opted for a Montgolfière but with an adaptation of his own. Where the French had used an open fire, he seems to have opted for a form of stove, which could be controlled by a simple damper. This would have allowed him to adjust the amount of hot air rising into the balloon. His first flight took off in the early morning from Christ Church Meadows on 4 October 1784 and he recorded rising to a height of 3,600 feet. Unfortunately, he lost the implement he was using for feeding his stove with fuel, so that inevitably the flight was a short one, landing between the villages of Woodeaton and Islip on the edge of Otmoor.

For his next venture he decided on a change of tactics, opting for a hydrogen balloon. Word of his earlier success had spread and this time a large crowd gathered on 11 November to see him take off from the physic garden, now known as Oxford's Botanic Garden. Once again, the wind took him out over Otmoor but this time pushed him along until he made a rough landing near Aylesbury. Sanders had not reckoned on the force of the wind, which dragged the balloon along the ground until the whole contraption ran into a tree. The balloon was destroyed, but Sadler emerged unscathed and ready to consider more flights. He definitely seems to have had trouble mastering the art of ballooning, not surprising considering how very few flights had been made by anyone at this time. He certainly seems to have been unaware of the dangers inherent in taking off on gusty days. He had problems maintaining an altitude and it was a brave man who would volunteer to join him on his flights. One who did was the prominent Whig politician William Wyndham, who wrote a letter to George James Chomondeley that was to be opened if he failed to return from the venture, in which he solemnly spoke of his Christian faith. They set off from Moulsey Hurst on the Thames for what turned out to be a very rough ride and when they finally landed near the mouth of the Medway, although they survived they were quite unable to control the balloon which floated away without them, eventually being picked up in the North Sea. He made four ascents in 1785, two of which ended in near disaster. On a flight from Manchester, the landing proved difficult and he was dragged along for two miles before he was eventually able to detach himself. A flight from Worcester was even worse; he was pulled along the ground for five miles before eventually falling out. The balloon, relieved of his weight, took off and was never seen again. Whether it was the alarming nature of his landings or the expense of losing the balloon, Sadler decided to abandon flying.

It is not clear where or how he developed a knowledge of chemistry, but he obtained a post as a chemical technician at Oxford University and began a series of experiments of his own, including the use of gas lighting and the development of steam powered road vehicles – an interest he was unable to pursue thanks to Boulton & Watt having a patent that gave them a virtual monopoly on steam engine development. In 1796 he was appointed as Chemist to the newly formed Naval Works Department, and while there he helped develop the table steam engine and devised a more accurate form of cannon. He was to return to ballooning later in life with a number of daring, pioneering flights. On one of these he was caught up in a gale and was swept along for over a hundred miles in an hour and twenty minutes at an average speed of over eighty miles an hour - which would either have been totally exhilarating or absolutely terrifying depending on one's temperament, It is safe to say that no human being had ever moved at such a speed before – and would not do so again for many years.

Sadler's most ambitious flight was an attempt to cross the Irish Sea on 1 October 1812. For this he constructed an especially large balloon 55 ft in diameter with such large capacity that he was able to carry an impressive load of ballast weighing over half a ton. He set off from Drumcondra in Ireland with the balloon two thirds inflated to allow for expansion of the gas. All seemed to go well, but a small tear in the fabric appeared. Sadler used his grappling rope to climb up and repair the slit and all was well as a favourable wind carried him over the Isle of Man. He made landfall over Anglesey at a height of 18,000 ft. Had he chosen to descend at that point he would have achieved his ambition, but he decided it would make a far greater impression if he continued his flight, aiming for the busy port of Liverpool. But the fates were against him; the wind direction changed and although he kept adjusting his height in the hope of finding a following wind, he was carried back out to sea. Eventually he was forced down in the Irish Sea near a Manx herring drifter, *Victory*. The skipper of the vessel managed to prevent the balloon drifting away by ramming it with his bowsprit and Sadler was safely brought on board. It had been a long flight of almost 300 miles, mainly over the sea, but ultimately, although he had flown over the Welsh coast he could not claim the crossing.

Sadler's sons John and Windham both followed their father into ballooning and it was to be the younger of the two, Windham, who was to achieve the feat that defeated his father. On 22 July 1817 he took off from Dublin and landed in Anglesey. It was an event that gave great satisfaction to the father, but the triumph was to be tragically short lived. On 20 September 1824 Windham took off from Bolton, but the balloon hit a chimney between Blackburn and Haslingden and the aeronaut fell to his death. James Sadler died just four years later. The Sadlers had achieved a great deal, survived some near disasters and deserve to be remembered as being among the great pioneers of ballooning.

CHAPTER FOUR

Coming of Age

A great deal had been achieved in the first two decades since the Montgolfiers had sent their first balloon into the air, but the future was still uncertain. No one really knew whether this interesting phenomenon represented a potential form of aerial transport or was merely a frivolous pastime for dilettantes. So why were so many intrepid men and women ready to risk their lives in such a dubious enterprise? There are two possible answers. The first is that there will always be those who want to push against existing boundaries and wish to have the honour of doing something that no human being had ever done before. There was also a more mundane reason: there was money to be made in ballooning. The two were not mutually exclusive. Few of the early aeronauts combined such a voracious appetite for both money and glory as Jean Pierre Blanchard.

He was born in Normandy in 1753 and early on in his life showed both a taste for mechanical inventions and a strong urge grossly

Pierre Blanchard's flight setting off from the English south coast for the first ever aerial crossing of the English Channel.

to overestimate his own achievements. At the age of sixteen he designed a velocipede, a four-wheeled vehicle that was worked by means of a foot treadle – an early forerunner of the bicycle. However, he was not satisfied with travelling on the ground and decided to adapt the principle of the velocipede to create a flying machine. Now the foot treadles were used to work two flapping wings and a further pair of wings were worked by hand levers. Blanchard boasted that his machine really had flown and that he had sped above the ground at high speed – but somehow never quite got round to demonstrating the contraption to anyone else. Blanchard may never have flown his winged velocipede, but he remained convinced of the value of wings. So when he heard of the successful balloon flights of the Montgolfiers and Charles he decided that he would build a balloon to take him aloft and add wings that would propel him in whatever direction he chose.

His first attempt at a flight got off to a very unpromising start. He had intended to take off with a Benedictine monk as his companion – whether as a friend or as a spiritual insurance policy is unclear. However, a young man called Dupont de Chambon appeared at the launch site in Paris, demanding to be allowed to join them. When he was refused he lost his temper, leapt into the car and slashed wildly about with his sword. He injured Blanchard's left hand, damaged one of the wings and attempted to cut through the rigging, before he was forcibly removed. After the attack, Blanchard decided he would make a solo flight and took off. He declared that thanks to his wings he would steer his balloon and land at La Villette to the north of Paris. The wind proved to be a rather more powerful force than the flapping wings and he ended up travelling for a short distance in the opposite direction, landing south of the capital. He made two ascents from Rouen, during which he claimed to have changed direction using the wings that he 'agitated with great force'. The truth was that his flights were far from noteworthy and there was only his own unsubstantiated account that recorded the success to be had from his wings. Blanchard decided that there were perhaps too many rivals – and rather more successful rivals – in France and decided to make his mark in England.

Blanchard was fortunate, for in England he found a group of wealthy enthusiasts for ballooning who were willing to pay his expenses and give him a fee for the privilege of flying with him. Among them were two eminent doctors, Dr John Sheldon and an American Dr John Jeffries. Sheldon was the first to pay for a flight and he brought along several scientific instruments in order to study meteorological phenomena. Blanchard brought his pet dog, a load of provisions and a basket of pigeons. The load proved too much and Blanchard simply threw several of Sheldon's instruments overboard, which could hardly have endeared him to the would-be scientist. However, it was enough to get the balloon moving from the launch site in Chelsea. The aeronaut was still convinced that he could power and steer his balloon using wings and he had now added what he called a 'moulinet' or small windmill. This was hand operated and must have been just about as useful as the flapping wings. It does, however, have a niche in aviation history as the first use of a propeller in the air, even though with no suitable power source it was quite useless. The balloon sailed north and Sheldon seems to have become thoroughly disenchanted with his arrogant pilot and was put down at Sunbury-on-Thames. Blanchard continued to fly on alone eventually landing at Romsey. Now that there was no one on board to contradict him, Blanchard made extravagant claims about the flight, saying that he had risen to previously undreamed-of heights. Sheldon had not abandoned the idea of ballooning and tried to persuade the Royal Society to promote further experiments, but without success. He was never, however, to contemplate flying again with Blanchard.

It was now Jeffries' turn to foot the bill. Things went rather better than before and the two men planned the most ambitious flight yet: the crossing of the English Channel. Sadler had hoped to be the first to gain this honour, but problems with the balloon had forced him to cancel the whole enterprise. For Blanchard this was to be the flight that was to cement his reputation as the world's greatest aeronaut – a distinction he was decidedly unwilling to share with anyone, and that included the man who was paying the bills. The balloon and the hydrogen apparatus were brought to Dover Castle and everything was ready for the flight. Blanchard tried to keep Jeffries away and when that scheme failed he announced that their combined weight would be too great for the flight and he would have to go alone. This was decidedly odd, as Blanchard appeared to have suddenly become heavier than he had been a day or two before. The ruse was easily discovered – he had a belt of lead weights under his coat. Jeffries must have been a remarkably good-natured man, and instead of withdrawing his backing from the enterprise as he could quite easily have done, seems simply to have laughed the whole thing off. Perhaps he thought the

A portrait of André Jacques Garnier with his parachute in the background.

enterprise too exciting to be cancelled just because of the petulant selfishness of his companion. So, on the morning of 7 January 1785, all the equipment was brought to the cliff edge and launched at 1 p.m. As usual with a Blanchard balloon it had the cumbersome wings and moulinet.

Dr Jeffries wrote a detailed account of the flight. Progress was slow and by the time they were no more than two thirds of the way across the Channel, they had used all their ballast in an effort to gain altitude, but they were still dropping steadily down towards the waves. Blanchard gave the order to jettison as much as possible. Among the items to go overboard were the useless wings and moulinet. The balloon still obstinately refused to rise and Blanchard threw out his great coat and Jeffries followed suit. The situation was getting so desperate that Blanchard even jettisoned his trousers and the two men put on their cork jackets in anticipation of a ditching. Just when the situation seemed hopeless, Jeffries noticed the barometer begin to fall and the balloon rose again. The situation was saved and they safely crossed the French coast. Jeffries described their landing which was, to say the least, interesting.

'We descended most tranquilly into the midst of the forest *De Felmores*, almost as naked as the trees, not an inch of cord or rope left, no anchor or anything to help us, nor a being within several miles. My good little captain begged for all my exertion to stop at the first tree I could reach. I succeeded beyond my comprehension, and you would have laughed to see us, each without a coat of any sort, Mr Blanchard assisting at the valve, and I holding on to the top of a lofty tree, and the balloon playing to and fro over us, holding almost too severe a contest for my arms. It took exactly twenty-eight minutes to let out air enough to relieve the balloon without injury. We soon heard the wood surrounded by footmen, horsemen, &c and received every possible assistance from them.'

In spite of the farcical elements of the aerial striptease it was an undoubted triumph, the first flight to cross the Channel. They were royally entertained and driven by an 'elegant chariot' to Calais where a large crowd greeted them. The aeronauts were presented to Louis XVI – presumably by then having been lent pairs of trousers, and the king awarded Blanchard a prize of 12,000 livres and a life pension. Jeffries had to be content with his share of the glory of being the first to fly the English Channel.

Blanchard continued his colourful career first by advertising the parachute he had designed and offering to give a demonstration of its usefulness. Wisely, he declined to try the device himself but instead used a dog for the experiment. It was not a success and the unhappy animal was killed in the fall. Blanchard was undeterred, and for his next venture used a cat, which survived the experience. But there was no suggestion at this stage that a human being might

M. S. BLANCHARD celebre aeronauta
al momento del volo aerostatico da Lei eseguito in Milano
in presenza delle LL. AA. II. e RR.
la sera del 15. Agosto 1811.

Sophie Blanchard
dressed in style, standing in the tiny gondola of her balloon, from which she would let off fireworks displays.

try and repeat the experiment. He then decided to make some money by opening a 'Grand Aerostatic Academy' with, his brochure assured potential visitors, grounds able to accommodate 'several thousand' carriages. They did not materialise and when various special spectacles were offered they proved equally unsuccessful – a sheep was supposed to be making a parachute jump but it never happened and an Italian promised to be the first human to use a parachute and declared that he would descend in style while playing a violin. In the event, he only dropped a few feet and had no time for even a single note. The crowd turned decidedly unpleasant, and Blanchard decided it was time to leave and return to France.

Blanchard may have had a touch of the charlatan in his makeup, but he did make a number of impressive ascents all over Europe, using both hot air and hydrogen balloons. During the French Revolution he was arrested in Austria, accused of spreading revolutionary propaganda, but he managed to escape and made his way to America. There he had the honour of making the first ascent in the New World. Altogether he made sixty ascents, but on the last he suffered from a heart attack from which he never fully recovered. He died in 1809.

One of the problems faced by all the early pioneers was that of controlling their flights, and there was a general agreement that, though the hydrogen balloon had many advantages, the montgolfière was easier to manage. So there seemed to be a possible solution to the problem: combine the two types to make a composite craft. It is generally agreed that the first attempt to create such a hybrid was the work of Pilâtre de Rozier. The enterprise was sponsored by the Comte de Provence and Jules Romain; the latter was responsible for the actual construction. It was intended to use it for a Channel crossing, starting from Boulogne. It was an ungainly contraption, with a spherical hydrogen balloon, 33 ft in diameter, below which was suspended the Montgolfière that was a cylinder 24ft high and 12 ft in diameter. The latter could only have provided minimum lift. The flying crew were housed in a gallery built round the cylindrical section and the iron fire grate was suspended beneath that. Rozier had only recently become engaged to an English girl, Susan Dyer, who begged him to give up the attempt. The only thing he would promise was that this would be his last flight.

After a long wait for suitable weather conditions, the balloon with Rozier and Romain on board finally set off early on the morning of 15 June 1785. Eyewitness accounts agreed that it appeared unstable form the first, with the gallery tilted at an angle. At first it drifted out to sea but a change of wind direction at a height of around 5000 ft sent it back over the land. It has never been quite certain what happened next, but there appears to have been a major problem. Rozier was seen to lower the fire basket as though to prevent a disastrous spread of the flames. But it was to no avail: the hydrogen caught fire and the whole contraption plummeted to earth. When the first spectators reached the wreckage Pilâtre de Rozier was dead and Romain was just able to gasp out the words 'O Jesu' before he too expired. Susan Dyer had witnessed the whole calamity and collapsed from shock; she never recovered and died a few days later, completing the tragedy of this doomed experiment. It inevitably reduced the enthusiasm for ballooning in France and in any case the whole country was thrown into turmoil in 1789 with the start of the French Revolution. In those desperate years there was, at first, no place for fripperies such as ballooning for pleasure; but enthusiasm remained undimmed in other parts of Europe. It was clear that any idea of controlling the direction of a balloon were, at that time at least, doomed to fail. The balloon was at the mercy of the winds – where they blew, it went. But it was also clear that people were enthralled by the sight of a balloon taking to the air and would be willing to pay. There were intrepid men and women who would be prepared to risk their lives in the hope of making fat profits.

There was no shortage of aeronauts making flights in Europe and America. The American Rufus Wells was almost certainly the most widely travelled, making flights not just in Britain and the United States, but also in South America, Egypt, India, Java, Japan and Australia. Men such as Wells were content simply to demonstrate flying in places that had previously never seen a balloon, but as more flights were made in Europe and America the population wanted something more than the mere spectacle of an aeronaut rising into the sky. Two French aeronauts, Lartet and Kirsch, developed a special balloon for displays. It was inflated on the ground using a very hot fire which enabled it to stay up long enough to carry acrobats aloft where they could perform tricks to amaze the crowd before sinking back to earth. Inevitably, however, the public became jaded with straightforward entertainment and demanded ever more exotic fare. There was no shortage of aeronauts ready to meet the demand. One balloon was fitted with a substantial platform, big enough to hold the French aeronaut Tétu-Brissy astride a horse. The same aeronaut made the first night-time ascent and others followed, letting off fireworks as they rose into the night sky – not one would have thought the safest thing to do with a hydrogen balloon. But the biggest attractions of all were the first real attempts by human beings to drop from a balloon by parachute.

André Jacques Garnerin was born in France in 1769 and showed a precocious interest in ballooning, making his first ascent from Metz at the age of nineteen. His aeronautical career was brought to an abrupt end by the French Revolution and the subsequent European war. He was enlisted as an officer in the army and sent to the front, arriving just in time for the regiment to lose a battle and the young soldier was captured by the English. He was handed over to the Austrians and imprisoned in a fortress at Buda in Hungary where he remained for over two years. As soon as he was released and returned to France he resumed his career in ballooning. Flights had lost some of their popular appeal, so if you wanted to attract a paying crowd it was essential to offer them a novelty. Garnerin's attempts began by making night flights, taking with him a lantern to illuminate the balloon. Anyone who has seen a nightglow at a balloon festival will know just how impressive an illuminated balloon can be. But he also had more ambitious plans. Together with his elder brother he designed a parachute system. He may have known of Blanchard's experiments of dropping animals by parachute, but he was proposing something far more daring. He would be the one to attempt to parachute down from a balloon at altitude.

Richard Cocking: the illustration on the left shows his parachute slung beneath the balloon; the picture on the right shows its tragic failure.

A large crowd gathered in the grounds of the Byron Hotel in Paris in June 1797 to see the leap into the unknown. Unfortunately, just as

the NASSAU BALLOON with The Parachute as it ascended.

M. COCKING.

the PARACHUTE as it descended by which M. Cocking lost his Life July 24 1837.

Garnerin was about to take off, a sudden gust of strong wind caught the balloon and did so much damage the flight had to be abandoned. Given that ballooning had been beset by several charlatans who had promised amazing things that they quite failed to deliver, the spectators took the cynical view that this was yet another con to take their money and the Garnerin brothers had to make a hurried and undignified exit. Three days later, however, they were ready for a second attempt. André climbed into a small basket, with the furled parachute attached above him. This whole arrangement was then itself attached below the balloon by a rope. At a height of 3000 feet, Garnerin cut the rope. The balloon shot skywards and was destroyed – according to an account by Wilfrid Fonvielle written in 1877 this was pre-arranged by Garnerin, presumably to ensure that there was no interference with the parachute. Whether deliberate or not – the parachute was now free and opened up like a giant umbrella 30ft in diameter. The descent, however, was far from comfortable as the basket was tossed backwards and forwards with the aeronaut clinging on for dear life. It did, however, do its job and Garnerin landed safely. He now had the honour of being the first human being to make a successful descent by parachute.

The problem he had with the wild swaying motion of the parachute was caused by the fact that it was made from impermeable material and there was no mechanism for spilling out the air. The astronomer Jérome de Lalande recognised the problem and wrote to Garnerin suggesting that for future drops he should arrange to have an opening at the top of the chute to prevent the problem recurring. If he took the advice it certainly doesn't seem to have helped. In 1802 he came to England and made his most daring descent yet. On 21 September he took off from London and this time rose to a height of 10,000 feet before cutting the rope and releasing himself and the parachute. The oscillations were even more alarming than on his French drop and the watching crowd seeing the mad gyrations feared the worst. In the event, he landed safely in a field at St. Pancras, badly bruised, very air sick but otherwise unharmed. The feat made its way into a broadsheet ballad with a piece of doggerel that was decidedly lame even by the often low standards of those publications.

'Bold Garnerin went up
Which increased his Repute
And came safe to earth
In his Grand Parachute.'

The parachute descents remained Garnerin's most impressive achievements, but he was to go on to have many eventful experiences over the years. A young lady, Mlle. Célestine Henry, begged to be allowed to join him for a flight. He was perfectly willing but at this stage the police stopped him on the grounds that they had been assured by august members of the medical profession that the female constitution was far too fragile to withstand the experience. Célestine seems to have been a lady of considerable character; she made it very clear to the authorities that the whole thing was entirely her own idea and she had every intention of flying. The authorities wilted under the pressure and she had her wish. What should have been one of his greatest public triumphs turned out, however, to be a public relations disaster.

The occasion was the coronation of Napoleon Bonaparte as Emperor of the French in December 1804. There was an immense celebration in Paris close to the cathedral of Notre Dame, with pageantry and fireworks. Garnerin's contribution was a balloon decorated with a slogan declaring it to be a celebration of Emperor Napoleon I and carrying aloft a great golden crown lit by coloured lanterns. It rose majestically and was enthusiastically cheered on its way. No one could have realised just how far this unmanned balloon would travel. It sailed away south and finally came to rest in Rome. That would not have been a problem had not the great golden crown of Napoleon landed on top of a statue of one of Rome's most notorious emperors – Nero. This was an absolute bonus for satirical writers all over Europe, who were able to draw comparisons between the famous Corsican and the equally famous but mad Roman. Although Garnerin could not possibly be held responsible for this extraordinary landing, he found himself out of favour and no longer the hero of the air.

The authorities may have tried to prevent Garnerin taking Célestine Henry as a passenger on one of his flights but another lady was to prove to be even more adventurous. Mme. Sophie Blanchard had taken over the work of her late husband, famous for his Channel crossing. Blanchard was an innovative balloonist but a poor businessman and in an attempt to arouse public interest and bring in more funds he decided to ask his young wife to accompany him – the spectacle of the young lady rising into the air would, he was sure, pull in the crowds. Whether or not it succeeded is not clear, but it delighted Sophie, who described the sensation of flying as incomparable. Her first ascent with her husband was at

Marseilles on 27 December 1804 and the following year she made her first solo flight from Toulouse. Perhaps the most remarkable thing about Sophie Blanchard was that everyone who knew her described her as being incredibly nervous – a loud bang terrified her and she was frightened of riding in carriages. Yet she was entirely fearless when it came to flying.

She carried on with her flying career after her husband's death. She had little choice as her husband's only legacy was his debts. She proved to have a talent for the spectacular. She regularly flew with a quite small hydrogen balloon and she rode in a variety of tiny baskets. She became so famous that following Garnerin's catastrophic fall from grace, she was appointed by Napoleon as the Aéronaut des Fêtes Officielles. In other words, she was officially in charge of organising flights at official ceremonies.

Mme. Blanchard became famous around Europe and made many remarkable flights, including a crossing of the Alps. While on a flight from Turin she flew so high that the temperature dropped to the point where icicles were forming on her hands. She regularly gave spectacular demonstrations at the Tivoli Gardens in Paris, a popular pleasure garden where patrons paid for admission and were rewarded by all kinds of entertainments, including balloon flights. On 6 July 1819 she made one of her night flights which,

A balloonists-eye view of London at Westminster, with the lake in St. James's Park a prominent feature.

as usual, would involve pyrotechnic displays. She was dressed in all her finery in a white dress and an ostrich plumed hat. The idea was that as she rose above the crowd she would light capsules of 'Bengal fire' which burned with brilliant coloured flames. According to contemporary accounts, she was worried about this particular flight but told well-wishers not to worry – it was to be her last big flight with fireworks. The balloon was slow to rise, but as soon as she was clear of the trees, she unfurled a large flag and began igniting the Bengal fire. It was then that disaster struck. No one saw exactly what happened but as the balloon emerged from behind a cloud it was seen to be on fire. It was losing gas rapidly but Mme. Blanchard was feverishly throwing out ballast to slow the descent. She might well have survived, but the balloon hit the top of a building and she was thrown from her flimsy perch and slid down the steeply sloping roof. She was unable to prevent herself from sliding over the edge and falling to her death into the Rue de Provence. The proprietors of the Tivoli Gardens donated that day's entrance fee for the support of her children and others collected money at the gate for the same cause – it was only later that it was discovered that she had no children. It was a sad end to the remarkable life of the 'very nervous' woman who had made 69 ascents. A memorial was erected in the Père Lachaise cemetery with a representation of the burning balloon and the epitaph that can be translated as 'Victim of her art and her intrepidity'. It is all too appropriate.

Sophie Blanchard was by no means the only fatality as aeronauts vied to offer ever more spectacular displays. It was a decidedly risky business. Lt. George Gale R.N. devised a system for making the firework displays much safer. He used two baskets, one fitting snugly inside the other. When he had reached an appropriate height, he lowered the outer basket and using a rope ladder clambered down with the fireworks that could now be let off safely well away from the inflammable hydrogen. The sight of him clambering down between the two baskets was almost as exciting as the fireworks themselves.

There were two specific problems with hydrogen balloons: the gas itself was very expensive to manufacture and it is highly inflammable. As early as 1784 the Belgian scientist J.P.Minielers had suggested using coal gas. This is a mixture of a variety of compounds, including carbon monoxide and methane that had originally been obtained when coal was burned in controlled conditions to produce coke for blast furnaces, but which would later be used for gas lighting. It was far cheaper to produce but far heavier than hydrogen so much greater quantities would be needed to provide an equivalent lift to that of hydrogen; measurements made at the end of the nineteenth century gave the weight of 1,000 cubic feet of hydrogen as 5 pounds and that of coal gas as 37½ pounds. One of the greatest enthusiasts for coal gas was the British aeronaut Charles Green who reckoned that he could fill six coal gas balloons for the same cost as just one hydrogen balloon. Nearly all his many ascents were made using coal gas. Like all pioneers he had his share of accidents and narrow escapes. One of the most dramatic took place on 19 July 1821.

The flight took place at Cheltenham with a reporter from the local paper called Griffith as a passenger. He was able to bring back a far more exciting story than he could ever have expected or wished for. As usual a crowd had gathered to see the event and milled around the basket before take-off. It was only when they were airborne that Green discovered that someone had slashed through one of the ropes holding the basket, so that it was seriously unbalanced. The extra strain on the remaining basket ropes was too great for them to hold and the two men were left clinging to the hoop. Then the net began to fail as well and Green made a hurried descent and tried to use the grappling iron to steady the balloon, but they were dragged along before the balloon eventually hit a tree, exploded and flung them to the ground. They survived the experience.

He thoroughly understood that to make any sort of impression a coal gas balloon would have to be bigger than anything yet manufactured. He designed a new balloon in 1835 based on many years' experience of some 200 ascents during which he estimated he had covered over 6000 miles. He could not afford to pay for the monster himself, but the funds were put up by the owners of Vauxhall Gardens and it was to be named the *Royal Vauxhall*. An order was placed with the silk weavers of Spitalfields for the manufacture of 2,000 yards of silk, manufactured from the raw material imported from Italy. The vast envelope was made up of alternating scarlet and white panels and instead of being stitched together they were fastened with a special chemical glue prepared by Green himself, and which he claimed would produce a far more robust envelope – as indeed it did. Once it was completed the balloon had a capacity of 70,000 cubic feet and when fully inflated rose to the immense height of 80ft. The car was a boat-shaped basket with gilded eagle heads at either end. Once the balloon had been tried and found to have far greater lifting power than expected, the boat was replaced by a larger, circular basket.

The maiden flight took place from Vauxhall Gardens watched by a large crowd that included the Foreign Secretary of the time, Lord Palmerston. The lift was so immense as it was filled that the 36 policemen who had been organised to hold it down proved hopelessly inadequate and an extra twenty workers had to be hastily recruited from the pleasure garden staff. Green was joined in the flight by his wife, his brother and six other passengers and in spite of it containing such a comparatively large and weighty group and the four hundredweight of ballast that was being carried, the balloon shot skywards at such a high speed that Green had to open the valve to release around 15,000 cu. ft of gas to slow the ascent. Even so in five minutes they had reached an altitude of around 13,000 feet. The flight was a great success and was soon followed by others.

One of the passengers on the maiden flight had been the M.P. for Hastings, Robert Holland and on a later flight he was joined by Thomas Monck Mason, an Irishman who had been a professional flautist and had composed a number of operas. The three men decided that they would like to use the great balloon to make an attempt on creating a long distance record for a balloon flight. The proprietors of Vauxhall Gardens agreed to give the flight their blessing. Green declared that the balloon could stay aloft for as long as three weeks – a decidedly optimistic estimate – and provisioned it with enough food to keep the three aeronauts from starvation – and enough drink to keep them permanently merry. The rations included 40 lb of various meats and the same weight of fowls and preserves; and 40 lb of sugar, bread and biscuits. They also carried two gallons each of sherry, port and brandy. With such a weight of provisions they needed only a modest 4 hundredweight of ballast.

The party left Vauxhall Gardens at 1.30 p.m. on 7 November 1836. As they passed over the Medway near Canterbury they dropped a message for the Mayor by parachute. It seemed that the wind was taking them out over the North Sea so Green decided to drop ballast in the hope that they would find a more favourable wind at a greater height. The plan worked and soon they were passing over Dover Castle, heading for the French coast. They sailed on into the night, which was moonless and impenetrably dark. Monck Mason in his book *Aeronautica* described the experience in very poetic language: 'we could scarcely avoid the impression that we were cleaving our way through an interminable mass of black marble in which we were embedded'. During the long, cold night the three men lost all sense of direction and as the sun rose they thought they might be somewhere over Poland or could have even travelled as far as Russia. They eventually landed at 7.30 in the morning after a flight of eighteen hours – not the anticipated three weeks. It was only after they had been met by enthusiastic locals that they discovered they were actually near the town of Weilburg in what is now Germany but was then the Duchy of Nassau. They had indeed created a new record by travelling 480 miles. They received a hero's welcome, were feted at balls and dinners and poems were written in their honour in both German and Latin. Green, however, had to organise getting the balloon back to Paris where it was to be exhibited and was henceforth to have a new name. It was to be the *Royal Nassau* balloon.

The flight was a triumph but not all Green's flights ended so successfully. On a flight of 24 July 1837, Green agreed very reluctantly to take up Richard Cocking and his experimental parachute. Cocking was born in 1776 and as a young man had seen Garnerin make the very first parachute descent and its alarming corkscrew descent. He was a professional watercolourist but a keen amateur scientist. He read an analysis of the problems faced by Garnerin in a paper *On Aerial Navigation* by George Cayley, who was himself to become a pioneer, not of ballooning but in developing heavier than air flying machines - gliders. In his essay, Cayley postulated that the oscillations could be avoided by using a parachute in the form of an inverted cone. Cocking at this time was 61 years old, had no flying experience of any sort, but nevertheless decided to have a parachute constructed that he would be the first to test. It was a vast device: the cone was 107 feet in circumference, connected by three hoops, and Cocking was to make his descent in a basket secured below it.

Cocking approached Green, who was reluctant to be a party to such a dangerous experiment, but the Vauxhall Gardens owners saw this as a spectacle that would attract great crowds. Green then made it a condition that he would not be the one to release Cocking and his parachute – he simply would not risk being responsible for sending a man to his death. So a device was arranged that would allow the parachutist himself to trigger the separation from the balloon. Responsibility for Cocking's fate was not the only worry that troubled Green. Once the weighty parachute and its occupant were released, the balloon was bound to shoot up in a totally uncontrolled fashion from the sudden loss of weight. He took suitable precautions. He added a second release valve so that he could vent gas, not just from the conventional position on the north pole but also from below the envelope. He was well aware that the gas could be asphyxiating if too much was released, so he also carried air bags with breathing tubes. He had done all he could to secure the safety of the balloon and himself and his companion on the flight, Charles Green Spencer. When all was ready, with the parachute slung beneath the balloon, they set off, rising slowly into the air, encumbered as they were with such a heavy load. At a height of 3,000 feet Green told Cocking that they were unlikely to rise any higher, at which Cocking calmly replied – 'Well, now I think I shall leave you' He triggered the release mechanism and dropped away out of sight.

The result was, just as Green had feared, almost calamitous as the balloon shot up and he described it in dramatic terms: the balloon was 'forced upwards with terrific violence and rapidity through unknown and untravelled regions, amidst the howlings of a fearful hurricane'. The two men left on board struggled to vent gas from both above and below the balloon but they kept soaring until they reached a level that according to the barometer was at a height of over 23,00 feet. At this altitude the two men must have found breathing difficult, but Green managed the situation perfectly and they were soon beginning a controlled descent to a safe landing in Kent. The one thing they did not know was the fate of Cocking after he had left them.

The large crowd that had come to watch the descent could see that Cocking was descending at a considerable speed. In his calculations he had allowed for a large enough parachute to hold his own weight – but had forgotten that the chute itself was also very heavy. The strain of the descent was too much for the fabric that began to disintegrate and at an altitude estimated as about 2-300 feet the basket became detached and Cocking fell to his death. The saddest part of the whole venture was that later experiments by an American, John Wise, showed that if Cocking had not neglected the weight of the parachute in his calculations and made a far larger canopy it would have worked quite safely. It did not, however, really offer any way forward. It was already almost too heavy for a balloon to carry and any extra weight would have rendered it quite useless. Although it was potentially more stable than Garnerin's umbrella-shaped chute, the problems of wild oscillations were easily solved by including a vent in the canopy. But Cocking's death did nothing to encourage any more speculative designs.

One of the most famous passengers to fly with Green was Henry Mayhew. His book, *London Labour and the London Poor* published in four volumes in 1851, was one of the first great sociological surveys ever carried out in Britain. The following year he took his flight and wrote an account in the *London Illustrated News*, a magazine to which he was already a regular contributor. He was now able to take an opportunity to view the London he knew so intimately at ground level from an entirely new perspective. He had, as he pointed out, become intimate with the London underworld and its depressing squalor.

'I had seen the world of London below the surface, as it were, and I had a craving to contemplate it far above it – to behold as it were, an angel's view of that huge city where, perhaps, there is more virtue and more iniquity, more wealth and more want huddled together in one vast heap than in any other part of the earth; to look down upon the strange, incongruous clump of palaces and workhouses, of factory chimneys and church steeples, of banks and prisons, of docks and hospitals, of parks and squares, of courts and alleys – to look down upon these as the birds of the air look down upon them, and see the whole dwindle into a heap of rubbish on the green sward, a human anthill, as it were; to hear the hubbub of the restless sea of life below, and hear it like the ocean in a shell, whispering to you of the incessant strugglings and chafings of the distant tide – to swing in the air above all the petty jealousies and heartburnings, and small ambitions and vain parades, and feel for once tranquil as a babe in a cot – that you were hardly of the earth earthy; and to find as you drink in the pure air above you, the blood dancing and tingling joyously through your veins, and your whole spirit becoming ethereal as, Jacob-like, you mounted the aerial ladder, and beheld the world beneath you fade and fade from your sight like a mirage in the desert; to find yourself really, as you had ideally in your dreams, floating through the endless realms of space, sailing among the stars free as 'the lark at Heaven's gate'; and to enjoy for a brief half-hour at least a foretaste of that elysian destiny which is the hope of all.'

Mayhew was clearly not a devotee of the short, snappy sentence, but he does at least convey the sense of wonder felt by those lucky few who took to the air in those early years of ballooning. He also managed to convey the strange sensations and experiences that anyone who has ever been in a balloon will recognise from their own very first flight. He describes the take-off: 'we shot into the air – or rather the earth seemed to sink suddenly down'. The other unforgettable experience is the landing. Mayhew's was certainly memorable.

> 'Suddenly the sound as of a gun announced that the bag had struck the soil, and then we were all told to sit low down in the car and hold fast. Scarcely had we obeyed the orders given than the car was suddenly and fiercely jerked half round, and all within it thrown one on top of another; immediately, after this, bump went the bottom of the car on the ground, giving us so violent a shake, that it seemed as if every limb in the body had been simultaneously dislocated. Now the balloon pitched on it side, and lay on the ground, struggling with the wind, and rolling about, like a huge whale in the agonies of death.'

The balloon eventually came to rest in a ditch and Mayhew ended his momentous flight sitting in a pool of water before locals appeared to help them out onto dry land. It had been an interesting if ultimately uncomfortable experience.

Green's final flight took place on 26 March 1870 and was advertised as his five hundredth, though he may well have made even more than that. He retired to his home in Highgate, London called, not surprisingly, Aerial Cottage. There he lived until he died peacefully at the age of eighty-five.

In this chapter we have looked at some of the most adventurous and innovative of the men and women who took ballooning into what some regarded as a golden age. But they all had one thing in common: they were not demonstrating any practical value in their profession, other than making money by charging others to enjoy the spectacle of flight. But there was a practical use and that appeared very early on in the history of aeronautics.

CHAPTER FIVE

Balloons go to War

When the French Revolutionary Wars began, the Committee of Public Safety in Paris considered the possibility of taking to the air. Their first notion was to make some kind of steerable airship, but when that idea failed, they turned instead to a much more practical notion. They decided that although balloons could not be controlled in flight on the other hand, if they were tethered to the ground they would be ideal observation posts from which to report on a battlefield. They formed the Compagnie d'Aérostiers – the Aerostatic Corps. The Corps was headed by a professional chemist Jean Marie-Joseph Coutelle, who was given the rank of Captain and an assistant, the engineer Nicolas Lhomond with the rank of Lieutenant. Apart from the two officers the entire corps was made up of just 26 soldiers. Coutelle was presented with a budget of 50,000 livres, part of which was used to purchase a balloon that was named *L'intrepide*. A new system of manufacturing hydrogen without sulphuric acid was also developed which saved a considerable amount of money.

There was a great deal of scepticism among the military hierarchy who at first saw little value in this new enterprise. Then, following the French victory at Charleroi that opened up their advance on the Low Countries, news came through of massive troop movements that suggested a planned counterattack by a combined Dutch-Austrian army. Battle was to be joined by the two armies, each numbering some 50,000 men near Fleurus in what is now Belgium. The French commander called on the Corps for assistance, only to discover that the balloon was thirty miles from the front, over a day's march. It was hastily inflated and then towed on a route march in time for the start of hostilities on 26 June.

Throughout the fighting, reports were sent down from the balloon using either semaphore or by dropping notes. Coutelle himself was in the observation balloon for a nine hour period constantly passing on messages. The crucial point came when the Dutch-Austrian army attempted a flanking movement to surprise the French but were easily seen from the high vantage point. The attack was repulsed in the ensuing battle; the French were victorious

An observation balloon rises high above the competing forces during a battle in the French Revolutionary Wars.

and their opponents withdrew. Inevitably there were some in the French army who claimed they would have won anyway, but to most independent observers it seemed to justify the value of having an aerial observation post. The authorities were, in any case, sufficiently impressed to form a second company, equipped with two more balloons. This second company was present at the Battle of Mainz and again at the retreat from Mannheim, again providing valuable information for the ground forces.

The original company continued to work with General Jourdan who had led the French at Fleurus. In September 1796 they took part in the Battle of Würzburg in which the French army was defeated and the entire corps was taken captive. The balloon was carried away as a trophy and is now on display in the Military History Museum in Vienna. The captured members of the corps were released on the signing of the Treaty of Loeben. They were to be deployed again during the Napoleonic Wars as part of the Egyptian campaign in 1798. Unfortunately, the ship that was to carry the balloons to France was attacked by the British Navy in the Battle of the Nile and they never reached their destination. In January 1799 the French government officially disbanded the Corps and the days of using balloons for observation on the battlefield were ended for many years. Historical 'what ifs' have no value in the real world, but it is still interesting to speculate what might have happened if Napoleon had been able to use the Corps at Waterloo. They would have seen Wellington's troops who, to the ground forces, were out of sight behind a ridge and Napoleon could have deployed his forces accordingly. But there was no Corps, no information and Napoleon's days of glory were ended.

More than half a century was to go by before balloons were again used in war, but this time across the Atlantic in the American Civil War. One of the most successful aeronauts of the day was Thaddeus S. C. Lowe. He was an ambitious man who had devised a massive balloon with a capacity of 725,000 cu. ft., with which he was convinced he could cross the Atlantic. There was a modestly successful trial flight, but on the next outing the monster was caught by a violent gust of wind before take-off and totally wrecked. At this point Lowe decided to make a more modest attempt at a long distance flight with his own much smaller balloon, *Enterprise*. His idea was to fly from his home town of Cincinnati to some distant point in the west. He set off on 19 April 1861, but as soon as he gained altitude he found the winds blowing him steadily south. He crossed the Appalachians and arrived in South Carolina where he decided to make a landing. He put down in a plantation, where the field hands and overseers greeted him as if he was a demon dropped from the sky rather than a mere human aeronaut. He decided it was prudent to take off again and try a different spot. The next plantation where he landed proved equally hostile and he had to draw his pistol to keep an angry crowd at bay. Convinced that he was not a demon, they now decided he was a Yankee spy and he was marched off to gaol. Fortunately, a local who had flown with him was able to convince the authorities of his innocence and he was able to make his way back north, unimpressed by the much-feted southern hospitality – the experience may well have had a bearing on his decision to offer his services to the Unionist cause when war broke out.

He brought his balloon to the White House, ascended to a height of 500 feet and telegraphed down reports of everything he could see that was happening in Washington DC. Abraham Lincoln was

Unionist forces
inflating a balloon
during the
American Civil War.

convinced by the demonstration and became one of the leading
proponents of the idea of having these valuable aerial lookouts. The
result was the formation of the Balloon Corps. Unlike the earlier
French corps this was a civilian organisation that was to be headed
by a 'chief aeronaut' appointed by the government. Several leading
balloonists applied but the job went to John Wise. In the summer of
1861 his balloon was accidentally destroyed during the first battle
of Bull Run at which point Wise became disillusioned and gave up
his post. The job was now handed over to Lowe who began a major
reorganisation and fundraising campaign.

Lowe made arrangements for seven balloons to be constructed, together with twelve gas generators to provide coal gas for inflation. He also arranged for an elderly steamer to be converted into a flat-topped barge so that balloons were not limited to use on land. It is sometimes referred to as the world's first aircraft carrier – though to classify static balloons as aircraft is stretching a point. From October 1861 the balloons were spread out along the Potomac river to provide an effective early warning system in the event of a Confederate attack on Washington. It was estimated that the observers would be able to spot any troop movement at least a day in advance of the enemy reaching the defensive line. That defensive role was soon to change. The General-in-chief of the Union Army, George B. McClellan, ordered his forces to advance on Richmond, the Confederate capital, and asked Lowe to scout ahead. He sent one of the Corps to Fort Monroe with a balloon but the weather conditions made it impossible to fly before McClellan's forces arrived. As the war spread Lowe recruited one of the best-known aeronauts of the day, James Allen, to join the Corps. He was instructed to follow the army as it advanced.

Lowe arrived at Hampden, Virginia on 28 March 1862 with all his equipment of balloons and gas generators aboard the flat-topped barge. He then continued by road to join the Union forces camped outside Yorktown. Here the army made a small group of about thirty men available to help him, and after a short training period they were able to make the first ascent of an observation balloon. A permanent balloon camp was set up by an old saw mill just a couple of miles from the Confederate occupied town. A second balloon post was established at General Keyes' headquarters on the James River. They were now able to oversee the Yorktown fortifications and keep an eye open for any movement of the ironclad steam-powered warship the CSS *Virginia* that was active on the James River, shelling Union positions.

Lowe made observations from the car below his small balloon *Intrepid* that had a huge portrait of General McClellan painted on it. This was no doubt very patriotic but must have encouraged the Confederates to attempt to shoot down such a tempting target. On 3 May Lowe was able to report there seemed to be a lot of movement on the Confederate side and shortly afterwards was able to send down the message that the fortress had been abandoned. It was time to move again with his barge loaded with equipment, moving up the Pamunkey River, a tributary of the York

A balloon being prepared for take-off that would carry the French politician Léon Gambretta away from besieged Paris to join the government in exile.

River, towards Richmond. It was here that the balloon observation post really proved valuable. Lowe took officers aloft one at a time so that they could familiarise themselves with the whole terrain. Lowe was not only able to look for enemy movement but was also able to direct artillery fire with great accuracy. In one engagement the gunners fired 96 rounds into a Confederate grouping near New Bridge causing heavy casualties and forcing the Rebel troops to withdraw. More importantly Lowe was able to report a massing of troops and warned McClellan that an attack was likely in the very near future.

The attack came on 31 May when General Joe Johnston engaged the Union forces in what became known as the Battle of Seven Pines. By this time the Confederates too had realised the value of observation balloons. Their first was constructed by Captain John Randolph Bryan. The Confederates had no supplies of acid, so it had to be a hot air balloon. The first trials almost ended in disaster; the balloon broke free of its tether and floated across the Confederate lines. The soldiers on the ground immediately assumed it was an enemy attack and began firing at it, fortunately for Bryan without success. A second balloon was then built, usually known as 'The Silk Dress Balloon'. Popular stories of the day had it that patriotic Southern ladies had sacrificed their best silk ball gowns to further the cause. The truth was less romantic; the balloon was simply made out of dress material. It was inflated and towed to the battlefield by a locomotive and then, as the fighting moved on, was drawn by a tug down the James River.

The battle was fierce and altogether three Union balloons were deployed to provide information. The result was indecisive, but it did have one important consequence. The Confederate leader General Joe Johnston was injured in the fighting and his place was taken by General Robert E. Lee, who was to prove a far more aggressive commander. It is, however, generally accepted that without the prior warning supplied by Lowe a surprise attack might have succeeded in driving out the Union forces. The two armies continued to face each other and the balloonists had some alarming experiences. James Allen was aloft in a balloon that was situated between the two main forces, with a small picket to protect him. To his alarm, he was able to spot a considerable number of Confederate soldiers advancing towards him and he was soon under fire. He ordered the balloon to be lowered, but it was going down so slowly and with the bullets humming past his ears he climbed out of the basket and shinned down the tethering line. Everyone got back to the safety of the Union lines.

Lee was ready to launch a fresh attack with the aim of driving the Union away from Richmond. As the attack moved forward it was clear that the balloon station at Gaines farm was under threat. It was hurriedly evacuated but two gas generators had to be left behind. A new station was established and Lowe was once again on duty, sending reports on the changing situation even though he declared himself to be ill and asked to be replaced. He could also look across the battlefield to where his opposite number, Porter Alexander, was sending flag messages to Lee from the Silk Dress balloon. Lowe described the scene as 'grand and picturesque beyond the compass of language' though it is doubtful if those below him found anything either grand or picturesque in the scene, as Lowe also wrote 'the ground had been fought over and consecrated with blood'. It was, in the event, to be a day won by the Confederates; the Union army and the balloonists were forced to withdraw. Lowe who had been complaining of feeling unwell, was diagnosed with malaria and sent home. He would never return to the army but while he was in control the Corps had made over 3,000 ascents in support of the army. The Corps was disbanded after the battle of Chancellorsville in 1863.

Porter Alexander summed up his own experience, which 'gave me the high idea of the possible efficieincy of balloons in active campaigns. Especially did we find, too, that the balloons of the enemy forced upon us constant troublesome precautions in efforts to conceal our marches.' While it is undeniable that the observation balloons played a significant role on the battlefield it was certainly not a decisive one. If other military experts were following events in America, they seem not to have been greatly impressed. When war again broke out in Europe between Prussia and France in 1870, there was no great enthusiasm for ballooning on either side.

Helmut von Moltke, the Chief of the German General Staff, did at least show an interest. The British balloonist Henry Coxwell was an early advocate of the military use of balloons and had given demonstrations of how they could be used to drop what were variously described as 'aerial torpedoes' or 'petards' and had included Berlin in the sites in which he demonstrated his ideas for aerial warfare in 1848. He also tried to interest the British Army in setting up a balloon corps by giving demonstrations at Aldershot in 1863. There was some talk about taking a balloon overseas to the Afghan campaign but nothing came of this, largely because of the difficulties of transport and means of inflation. Nevertheless, von Moltke called on Coxwell for help in his campaign. He was authorised to bring two balloons and two detachments of men to help at the siege of Paris in 1870. The balloons were sent but there was no generating equipment, so they were sent back to Germany and the whole enterprise was abandoned. On the French side the Minister of War had simply decided that balloons were useless. Nevertheless, two private balloons were sent up at the start of the siege but offered no help to anyone as visibility was far too poor. The situation changed dramatically, however, once the Prussian forces had completely surrounded the city and all land communication between Paris and the rest of France was cut off.

M. Rampont, the Director General of the Post Office, suggested that the only way they could communicate with the provisional government in Tours was by sending mail out by balloon. The idea was accepted and the task of making the first delivery was entrusted to a professional aeronaut, Jules Duruof. He was given 227 lb of mail to carry but he had only a rather old and somewhat leaky balloon to use for the task. He realised that if he was to clear the Prussian lines safely he would have to make a very rapid ascent so as to be out of gunshot range before the troops on the ground were alerted.

An observation balloon being prepared by British soldiers at Ladysmith in the Boer War.

The scheme worked. As the balloon was released, Duruof threw out a vast quantity of ballast and shot skywards. It was an audacious flight and the Prussians could do nothing about it. Just to annoy them even further, he dropped a shower of his visiting cards down on to their troops. After a flight of three and a quarter hours he made a safe landing well behind the enemy lines and the mails could now be forwarded by more conventional means.

It was not entirely satisfactory as a means of communication – it allowed outgoing mail to reach its destination, but there was no provision for incoming mail and replies. While it was possible for a balloon to leave Paris and cross the Prussian lines, there was no way in which a balloon could be guaranteed to fly from other parts of France and land in Paris – and even if it did it would be an easy target as it came in to land. A solution was supplied by a Parisian pigeon fancier called Van Roosebeke: the balloon leaving Paris would carry homing pigeons who would then fly back with important messages. On the next flight out of Paris, the usual heavy load of mail was carried with three of the pigeons that did indeed return safely with messages from the exiled government. This was only a partial solution to the problem; balloons and aeronauts were going out but not returning. The supplies of both these commodities were simply running out. The last privately-owned balloon piloted by Gaston Tissandier left Paris at the end of September. But the authorities could see by now how vital this service was and they took urgent steps to remedy the situation.

There was an urgent need for suitable workspaces where balloons could be manufactured on a large scale and it was the nature of the siege itself that made just such spaces available. With all land communications cut off, the city's railway stations were empty and available, so workshops were at once established at the Gare du Nord and the Gare d'Orléans. Bales of balloon cloth were brought in and a small army of seamstresses was employed, some having the use of sewing machines and the rest stitching by hand. Sailors were brought in to make the nets. The postal department was in charge of the operations and an efficient production line was set up. Each station produced comparatively large balloons of 70,000 cubic feet capacity but they had distinctive features: balloons from the Nord were white, those from Orléans multi-coloured.

The balloons off the production line all had names and the first was named after one of the leading revolutionaries of nineteenth century France, Armand Barbès. It was to be used not specifically for mail but to carry a very important passenger, Léon Gambetta. He was an ardent republican who, when Sedan fell to the Prussians, demanded the overthrow of the emperor and the establishment of a new Government of National Defence. He could do nothing useful holed up in Paris and the idea was to enable him to join his government colleagues in Tours, where he was to be Minister of the Interior. The balloon in which they were to travel was smaller than the usual production at just 50,000 cubic feet and the pilot Trichet had a problem getting sufficient height when crossing the Prussian lines. As a result, they came under fire and Gambetta was shot in the hand. They came down in a field perilously close to the Prussians but managed to make good their escape. Like the other balloonists they carried pigeons and were able to send back a message to say that Gambetta had arrived safely in French controlled territory.

The lack of professional balloonists in Paris, as one by one they disappeared on their one-way missions, was a serious problem. It was decided to train sailors to fly the balloons, presumably with the idea that anyone who could control a ship under sail might be able to cope with its airborne equivalent. The men could only receive the most rudimentary of training but the scheme worked well. What was less satisfactory was the system used to bring the messages back to Paris. Obviously, there is a limit to what a pigeon can carry, so the messages were photographed and reduced in size so that up to 300 short items could be included on a single sheet of paper. They could then theoretically be read using a powerful magnifying glass. Unfortunately, they often proved very difficult to read and were sometimes totally undecipherable. There was an alternative. René Dagron had invented a microfilm system that he patented in1859 – the very first microfilm patent. With this system a pigeon could carry six films containing up to 5,000 letters. Inevitably there was a snag. Dagron had the only equipment able to make the films – and he was in Paris. So, like Gambetta, he had to be flown out – and like Gambetta only just escaped capture on landing. But soon a regular supply of microfilmed reports was arriving back in Paris.

As balloon fights became ever more frequent the Prussian efforts to stop them increased and word reached Paris that the enemy had a new, more powerful weapon that would be able to hit a balloon even if it flew at its normal height over their lines of around 3,500 feet. It was decided to play safe and only fly at night. Given that inexperienced sailors rather than professional balloonists were now manning the flights, it might be thought that they would have been better off braving Prussian fire power. Balloons often finished up in the most unlikely places: the first night flight ended up in Holland and one balloon made it all the way to Norway. Two balloons were lost and never seen again, though one of them was spotted over Cornwall heading out cross the Atlantic. Six others were captured, one of them landing in Munich. But 58 made successful flights, carrying a total of two and a half million letters and 400 pigeons. The operation was an undoubted success and must have infuriated the Prussians – and they were made even more frustrated by the fact that as the balloons sailed over their heads the soldiers on the ground were showered with propaganda leaflets.

The siege ended in 1871 when the Prussians finally took Paris, but it was obvious that balloons were now an essential part of any campaign, both for observation and communication. The French established a permanent Commission des Communications Aerienes in 1874 and were later followed by Germany, Austria and Russia. As mentioned earlier Coxwell had demonstrated a balloon to the army at Aldershot but the military authorities of Britain were famously conservative and showed no interest. It was not until 1878 that Captain James Lethbridge Brooke Templer, who held a commission in the militia, persuaded the authorities to establish a balloon school and a manufacturing centre. His was in a curious position, neither a full time military officer nor a full time civilian. He was, however, a balloon enthusiast and to get the new organisation started he brought his own balloon, the *Crusader*, to the Woolwich Arsenal to get the new organisation going. He had a team of Royal Engineers under his command and together they produced a number of major advances in balloon design and use.

One of the problems on which the team worked was the economic production of hydrogen. Various ideas were tried and for a long time it seemed the best answer was to use sulphuric acid with granulated zinc. Later he turned to a very different technology – the electrolysis of water. They also devised a means of storing the gas under pressure in cylinders. Up to that time, balloons had mostly been made out of light material such as silk, which then had to be varnished to make it gas-tight. Templer wanted a lighter material and turned to goldbeaters' skins – the material was actually made from the intestine of cattle. By using this very light material he was able to use quite small balloons to lift observers.

Templer and his crew soon left Woolwich to establish a balloon school at Chatham. In order to fly the balloons, he hired land on a nearby farm at his own expense. Strictly speaking there was no need for any of the trainees to know about free flight, since all they were ever expected to do was act as observers from tethered balloons. Templer, however, declared they should learn the rudiments of flying in case their machines broke loose from their moorings. He also, as a keen aeronaut himself, realised that the men would soon get bored being permanently anchored to the ground and actual flights would increase their enthusiasm for the job in hand. There was to be one further move to Aldershot where an area in the grounds was named Balloon Square.

Templer was involved in one balloon tragedy. On 10 December 1881, he set off with two passengers – Walter Powell, the M.P. for Malmsbury and A. Agg-Gardner, whose brother had recently been M.P. for Cheltenham. They left Bath and their flight took them towards the Dorset coast near Bridport. It was obvious that they would be soon heading out to sea, so it was decided to come down as quickly as possible. The balloon touched down just 150 yards from the cliff edge. Templer jumped out holding the valve line in his hand and called on the others to abandon the basket. Lightened of its load the balloon was now some eight feet above the ground. Agg-Gardner jumped out and fell awkwardly, breaking his leg. Powell, however, seemed reluctant to risk the leap, but Templer was finding it increasingly difficult to hold the line, while the injured Agg-Gardner was in no condition to help. Eventually, as the line cut deep into his hand, he was forced to let go. The balloon rose with Powell still aboard and disappeared out to sea. Neither it nor Powell were ever seen again.

Observation balloons were to be used by the British in a number of campaigns most notably during the Boer Wars. Three detachments were sent to South Africa, one of which was used in the siege of Ladysmith and others in the advance on Pretoria. One of the main difficulties the army faced was transporting all the equipment, often having nothing more effective than lumbering bullock carts. Rather surprisingly the South Africans reported seeing airships floating over their ranks in the Transvaal. Quite what they did see was a mystery. There were no balloons in that area and airships were still no more than a dream of the future.

CHAPTER SIX

Experiments and Expeditions

It was all very well for aeronauts to undertake public flights, accompanied by entertainments such as acrobats and fireworks, but there were some who dreamed of far greater feats. They could, they believed, design balloons that would travel great distances if only they could be made big enough. Many proposed giant balloons were so fanciful that even if they had ever left the drawing board could never have flown. One that did was the brainchild of an Englishman, J.W. Hoar. He constructed an enormous hot air balloon that when inflated stood at a height of 130 feet. The launch was planned for 24 May 1838. It was inflated from a platform in the middle of the pond in Surrey Zoological Gardens. The date was chosen because it was Queen Victoria's birthday and the balloon was christened *Queen's Royal Aeronaut* though it is far from clear that the monarch had any idea that her name was being used. As usual a large crowd of paying spectators had gathered for the event but when the launch time appeared, the balloon remained firmly attached to its mooring. The crowd became increasingly restless and in the early evening a boat appeared on the lake with a placard announcing there would be no flight, but there would be a fireworks display. The London crowd had seen too many ballooning charlatans over the years and simply assumed this was another. They turned angrier and angrier and soon missiles of all kinds were being hurled at the great balloon until eventually it was reduced to shreds.

Hoar was obviously a man of optimistic temperament who refused to be put off by the fiasco. A second balloon was constructed and this time the flight was to coincide with the opening of the Croydon Atmospheric Railway, which was not inappropriate – a doomed aeronautical experiment to coincide with the launch of an equally flawed railway system. The attempt was no more successful than the first.

Hoar's failure did not deter others and among the dreams of the more adventurous aeronauts was the prospect of crossing the Atlantic by balloon. America laid claim to the first successful Atlantic crossing, when a *New York Sun* account informed readers

Nadar, resplendent in top hat, was the first man to take photographs from the air.

that Monck Mason had arrived in South Carolina after launching from Great Britain. Alas, the story was a hoax but a convincing one, as it had actually been written by one of the country's most inventive authors, Edgar Allen Poe. The story had some credence, for Americans had been planning an Atlantic crossing. An immigrant from England, Richard Clayton, had appealed for funds for a giant balloon he was creating for the flight, but if built it was no more successful than Hoar's had been. Another appeal was made in 1843, this time by John Wise, which proved more successful, and a financier, O.A. Gager, provided the funds. One reason for his success would be that he had already established a considerable reputation, not just because of the number of flights he had made but also because his inventiveness was well known. He devised a system whereby if the balloon was punctured it would automatically turn itself into a parachute, as the bottom half would fold up to create a canopy. He had probably never intended to put it to the test, but during a flight in 1818 his balloon did indeed puncture and the parachute worked – after a fashion. During the descent it oscillated wildly and fell far faster than the inventor had expected. On landing he was thrown ten feet into the air but survived more or less unscathed. The parachute had almost certainly saved his life. He also devised rip panels that could be opened to allow gas to escape for a controlled descent without having to rely on the valve at the top of the balloon. He realised that the balloon would be warmed by the sun's rays, saving on fuel and painted it black to reinforce the effect. He also used his flights for scientific research and described a 'great river of air that flows from west to east'. We now know this as the jet stream, but it was this reliable wind that persuaded him that an Atlantic flight was possible.

Wise was able to build his balloon and he made an experimental flight in the 50,000 cu ft balloon, optimistically named *Atlantic*. With a view eventually to making his trip across the ocean, a light lifeboat was slung beneath the car. His first flight, with three companions, took place in 1843, and almost ended in disaster. They took off from St, Louis and en route they were hit by a sudden storm that threatened to deposit them into Lake Erie. Wise decided that it was more prudent to jettison the lifeboat to gain height rather than land in the stormy waters. The plan worked and they eventually landed in Jefferson County, New York, having covered a very impressive 809 miles in just under twenty hours. In many ways it was a highly successful flight but it stretched Wise's abilities to the utmost and he abandoned the idea of the much more dangerous Atlantic crossing. It did not, however, prevent him from continuing with his flying career and among his other achievements was the first airmail delivery in America.

Wise was not the only well-known aeronaut in America to have ambitions of making a transatlantic flight. Thaddeus Lowe set about building an enormous hydrogen balloon for his attempt. It was even bigger than Wise's, standing 200 feet high and with a capacity of 725,000 cubic feet. Originally known as *City of New York* it was later renamed *Great Western*. Like Wise, Lowe carried a lifeboat, powered by a steam engine that could either be used to work paddles or a steam propeller – perhaps inspired by the arrival in New York of the other *Great Western*, Brunel's pioneering iron ship, the first vessel to cross the ocean powered by propeller. Lowe also intended to use the propeller to help with navigating his monster through the airways. The first trial flight from Philadelphia in June 1860 ended in New Jersey on the very day that Brunel's latest and largest ship, the *Great Eastern*, arrived in New York. It was after this attempt that Lowe made his flight that ended in the deep south, described on pages 69 to 73. In the event Lowe, like Wise, thought better of the whole idea and abandoned all plans for crossing the ocean. Other Americans took up the challenge, one of whom, Samuel King, made his attempt in a balloon that was said to be the first to have a capacity of a million cubic feet. Alas, it proved no more successful than any of the others, its maiden flight being more of a short hop than a lengthy journey. But the idea of building big to cover long distances was not restricted to the United States. European aeronauts soon joined the fray.

Gaspard-Félix Tournachon was born in Paris in 1820 and originally planned to have a career as a doctor. He paid for the first year of training by writing theatre reviews and discovered that he found journalism rather more pleasing then medicine. He developed a growing reputation as a political and satirical cartoonist and

A ticket to see the launch of the massive balloon *L'Aigle.*

adopted a pen name. His first choice was Tournachon, which could be translated as 'one who stings' reflecting the sharpness of his satires. But he changed and shortened that to Nadar, the name by which he is now generally known. In the 1850s he developed a new interest in the growing practice of photography and was to become famous for his portraits of many of the most notable people of his time, ranging from Wagner to Victor Hugo. He also photographed his friend, Jules Verne, well known for his futuristic stories and visions of advanced technologies. The two men developed an interest in balloons and speculated on what new possibilities they might open up. Nadar was certainly impressed by his own first flight where he described the ascent as 'being free, calm, levitating into the silent immensity of welcoming and benign space'. He also realised that his elevated viewpoint offered an opportunity to give the world at large a new perspective: he would attempt to take photographs from his gondola. He had problems at first in stabilising the balloon to keep the camera steady, but once he had solved that problem he was able to produce the world's first aerial photographs, including views over Paris taken in 1858.

Nadar was convinced that eventually flight using propeller-driven heavier than air machines would be possible. In the meantime, however, he knew of no mechanism by which such a machine could be lifted into the skies other than by means of a giant balloon. First of all, he would need to make the balloon and test it out. The result was appropriately known as the giant, *Le Géant*. It stood 196 feet high and was constructed from 22,000 yards of fine silk. It was a remarkable sight, but even more remarkable was the gondola, an immense wickerwork constriction measuring 13ft by 8ft and divided into various compartments. It was clearly designed for what Nadar hoped would be long flights, with a cabin for the captain and a three-berth cabin for passengers. There was a provision store and two compartments for Nadar's photographic equipment and a small printing press. It even boasted a separate compartment for a lavatory and the roof had a balustraded balcony so that the aeronauts could be out in the open to control progress and enjoy the view. As landing such a monster safely was clearly going to be problematic, it was supplied with a pair of axles and four detachable wheels.

The first ascent took place, as so many pioneering flights had in the past, from the Champ de Mars in Paris in October 1863 and, not surprisingly, attracted a large crowd. Nadar was to be the captain with his two brothers to assist him and there were plans for twelve passengers. Nadar had firmly declared this was to be a male only enterprise, but when the young and attractive Princess de la Tour de Avignon pleaded with him to be allowed to join he was unable to resist. In the event it was something of an anti-climax. The balloon took a very long time to fill and when it finally got airborne late in the afternoon it came to rest just fifteen miles away. The passengers who had all brought passports along having been assured they would be carried well clear of the French borders literally came to earth with a bump. The gondola was tipped on its side and dragged along for about a mile. Later investigation indicated that the problem was a constant leak of gas from the valve.

Once that problem had been sorted out, a second flight seemed to be going off spectacularly well. With six passengers on board, including Nadar's wife, they sailed away from Paris. As the sun set they gathered on the balcony and enjoyed fine wines courtesy of a Parisian wine merchant who had given them six cases, which should have been quite enough for even the longest journey they were contemplating. They sailed on through the night, crossing first into Belgium and then into the Netherlands. At this point they seemed to be heading for the North Sea, and Nadar's brothers suggested they ought to land rather than be carried out over the water. Nadar, however, felt that the risk of a night landing outweighed any other dangers. He was lucky, for the wind changed direction and began carrying them off towards Germany. The River Ems was crossed in brilliant sunshine that made everything seem very pleasant for the passengers, but worried Nadar. The heat was causing the fabric of the envelope to expand and he feared that unless urgent action was taken it might burst. He decided to descend.

A fact that all balloonists have to be aware of is that air currents vary depending on the altitude. Riding high over the land they had enjoyed a gentle breeze to waft them along in their stately progress. But as they neared the ground they found a strong wind blowing and by this time so much gas had been released during the descent that there was nothing to be done: the vast balloon continued on its unstoppable descent until it hit the ground. As soon as it landed the fabric began to act as a giant sail and the unhappy crew and passengers found themselves racing at high speed across the countryside, often proceeding like some giant kangaroo in a series of hops. Attempts to use the grappling irons proved useless; the first was simply torn from the balloon while the second took away part of a roof. Still the mad journey continued and what seemed like inevitable disaster loomed in front of them. They were heading straight for a railway line and there seemed every possibility that they would arrive at precisely the same time as the locomotive puffing its way down the tracks. Fortunately, the driver had seen the danger and managed to bring his engine to a halt. He was able to watch as the strange apparition crossed right in front of him, demolishing a telegraph pole and dragging its wires behind as it went. Eventually, everything came to a halt when the flying balloon finished up hitting the edge of a patch of dense woodland. By this time Mme Nadar was the only passenger still on board, the rest were all scattered in the wake of the careering balloon. Amazingly, all survived. Had the balloon been fitted with Wise's rip panels, Nadar would have been able to release the remaining gas, deflate the balloon and collapse it. In spite of his alarming experience, Nadar continued to fly but never made such a long flight again.

The search for a way to make long distance flights resulted in the design of ever larger balloons. The biggest ever built at this time was designed by Eugène Godard with a capacity of 500,000 cubic feet. Godard also designed an immense metal stove that was eighteen feet across and weighed almost a thousand pounds. This was surrounded by a gallery to hold the aeronauts and passengers. The stove was embossed with the figure of an eagle and that gave

The Andrée Polar expedition balloon in its temporary shelter, part of which has been removed ready for take-off.

the balloon its name – *L'Aigle*. He flew the monster in England, taking off from the Cremorne pleasure gardens in Chelsea. There were two ascents but neither made much progress. Others took up the challenge.

Henri Giffard was an engineer with his own works in the Avenue de Suffren in Paris and he decided to make a very large hydrogen balloon for the Paris Exhibition of 1867. Unlike the other large balloons this one was never intended to go anywhere. It would be permanently tethered and would be used to give visitors to the exhibition a chance to ascend safely, experience the excitement of ballooning and then be returned smoothly to the point where they started. Needless to say, Giffard charged them for the privilege; this was primarily a money-making exercise. Following the success of that experiment, he took the balloon to the Paris Hippodrome and was then persuaded to cross the Channel and offer the same entertainment to the citizens of London. Once again the site chosen was by the Cremorne Gardens, but the first balloon, given the appropriate name *Captive* was irreparably damaged by workmen, and Giffard had to start again to construct a new, even larger version of 424,00 cubic foot capacity. The enterprise was not the success that had been hoped. Londoners seemed nervous and their enthusiasm was finally squashed completely following an unfortunate accident. The balloon was tethered by 2,000 feet of steel cable that ran through a pulley to a steam winch. Due to a mistake by the winch operator, the cable caught in the pulley and snapped, releasing the monster into the skies where it shot up to a height of over ten thousand feet. The basket could have been holding up to thirty passengers, but fortunately it was empty. However, the sight of the escaping behemoth was enough to confirm all the Londoners' fears. The experiment was brought to an end, but it was not the end for Giffard's balloon.

Wilfrid de Fonvielle persuaded Giffard to allow him to use the balloon for free flight to promote a proposed polar expedition and renamed it *Le Pole Nord*. He wanted to prove that a vast balloon could indeed be used for long flights and he prepared for the adventure with his companion, the experienced aeronaut Gaston Tissandier and two other men, by stocking up with 'essential' supplies, including sixty pints of wine and twenty of brandy. As with so many other attempted long flights they never got very far, setting down in Auneau near Chartres. The one positive aspect of this flight was that Tissandier made a perfectly controlled landing instead of suffering the fate of Nadar and his crew. Locals helped secure the balloon and also assisted in demolishing the copious quantity of drinks on board. After that Giffard returned to making balloons for tethered flights, with his largest effort yet with a capacity of 883,000 cubic feet. This enabled him to take 52 passengers on each ascent and during its stay in Paris, some 35,000 visitors took to the skies.

There were still aeronauts who had ambitious plans for long distance flights and none was more ambitious than Solomon August Andrée who planned to fly across the Arctic, crossing the North Pole along the way. He made his first balloon flight at the Philadelphia World Fair at the age of twenty-two and became an instant enthusiast. He made a number of spectacular flights, including crossings of the Baltic Sea and became an expert aerial photographer. In 1895 he announced his intention of mounting the polar expedition, a suggestion that was met with considerable scepticism. Andrée, however, had done his homework. He pointed out that in that region the winds were steady and he could count on a northerly blowing for at least two weeks duration. By taking off in the summertime when there was almost constant daylight, there would be very little variation in temperature, which meant that the gas in the balloon would remain more or less at the same pressure. He also planned to increase the speed and control the direction of his flight by attaching a sail. He experimented with a balloon called *Sven* and used trail ropes that could be dropped down to drag along the ground to reduce the rate of ascent when necessary.

Once he was satisfied that the whole scheme really was practical, he applied for funds and attracted support from a number of eminent Swedes including Alfred Nobel. The expedition balloon, known in English as *The Eagle*, had a slightly elliptical shape and a capacity of 170,000 cubic feet. The upper half was fabricated from three layers of silk, the lower from a double layer. The valves, instead of being in the usual position at the top were set in the sides to avoid them getting blocked by snow and ice. The crew were housed in a double-decker wicker car with three sleeping berths and there was room for all their stores, as well as three sledges and a canvas boat as a precaution against a forced landing. The flat roof, surrounded by canvas, was to be used as an observation platform. There were three trail ropes, each over a thousand feet long. Andrée calculated that the balloon would be pulled down by ten feet for each twenty feet of rope dragging along the ground, so that he should be able to maintain an optimum altitude of between six and seven hundred feet. It all sounded as if it had been very thoroughly organised and the expedition set off for Danes Island, Spitzbergen on 31 May 1896.

The first requirement was to protect the precious balloon by building a temporary shelter round it with removable panels for when it was ready for inflation and ascent. Unfortunately, the 'reliable' northerly wind never materialised and after six weeks they were forced to return to Sweden, leaving the balloon and equipment behind them. The next year, however, they were back, once again with the financial backing of Alfred Nobel. The Swedish government provided a gunboat to take them to the island and also provided a crew to repair the hangar, dig the inflating equipment out of the snow and help prepare for the launch. Andrée's companions were Knut Fraenkel, an engineer with considerable experience of both the Arctic and engineering and Nils Strindberg, who among his other accomplishments was an expert photographer. Part of the car could be blacked out to act as a dark room and the idea was that photos of their progress could be sent back to base by carrier pigeon. Thirty-six of these birds were housed in special cages.

There was a problem with the balloon that leaked from some of its seams and attempts were made to patch it up, not entirely successfully. Even so the three men all agreed that this time they would set off. At a quarter to three on the afternoon of 11 July 1897 they climbed aboard and Andrée gave the order to cut the rope. A sailor took out his knife and sliced through the restraining line, nicking his finger. 'Oh Hell!' he exclaimed. 'That's where we're going' said Andrée as the balloon lifted off. The words were to be sadly prophetic.

The start did not go well. The sail was set and at once the balloon began wobbling from side to side. As it drifted along the shore one of the trailing ropes snagged in a rock, hauling the balloon down until the bottom of the wickerwork car was touching the water. Then the line snapped and the balloon sailed away to the north. It was never seen again.

In August 1930, the crew of a Norwegian sealer went ashore on White Island, a deserted stretch of land off the northeastern corner of Spitzbergen. It was there that they discovered three bodies and a great deal of equipment. The skipper was in no hurry to return to port as he was enjoying a very profitable voyage, but he passed on the information to Captain Jensen of the *Termingen* as the two boats passed each other and it was only when Jensen returned to port that the outside world heard of the discovery. At first there was some doubt as to whether these were the missing aeronauts or not, but an expedition to the island soon proved beyond doubt that it was indeed them. The equipment was quickly recognised. The skeletons of Andrée and Strindberg were identified, still wrapped in furs, but it was some weeks before the third member was found. He had clearly been the first die, for he had been buried in a shallow grave. The most exciting discovery was the expedition diary; it was now possible to piece together a picture of that fatal flight.

At first everything went well and messages were sent out by the carrier pigeons recording their progress. They were heading north at a good speed, the weather was brilliant and spirits were high. On the third day another pigeon was despatched still recording good progress – the last one that actually arrived back. Again, it recorded all was well. But that day things began to change. The men could hear the ominous crackle of ice building up on the fabric, occasionally breaking off in small sheets, but inexorably forcing the balloon ever lower. Eventually it was scarcely moving above ground level, so low that it kept running into hummocks of ice on the ground that sent it bouncing back up again, only to sink back down until the next jolt. On 14 July their luck seemed to have turned as for some reason the balloon suddenly rose up again, but it was only a respite. The constant bouncing and dragging over the ice had irreparably damaged the fabric and now the men could hear the hiss of escaping gas. By 7 p.m. that day there was no alternative; the rip valves were opened and they landed on the ice. They still had all their equipment, including the sledge, boat and ample supplies and on August 4 they set off to try and walk to safety. They plodded on for two weeks, only managing to cover sixty miles and were bruised, battered and suffering from frostbite. But eventually they reached open water and were able to use the canvas boat. They floated on for days and eventually on 17 September they sighted White Island and solid land. They celebrated the killing of a seal on the twentieth, and Strindberg's diary recorded this strange event: They feasted on 'seal steak, seal liver, seal brains, seal kidneys, butter, and Swedish bread, gateaux aux raisins with raspberry sauce, and port wine for dessert'. The latter had been a gift from the King of Sweden, whose health they drank. Eventually after terrible hardships, they reached White Island. Theoretically they had enough supplies to last them until the winter set in, the sea ice froze and they could sledge to safety. But they were too weakened by their ordeal. Strindberg's death was recorded as a 'heart attack' and shortly afterwards it seems the other two succumbed, simply too exhausted to carry on. It was to be the last great attempt to undertake a great balloon expedition of the nineteenth century. But there were other forms of exploration that also attracted the intrepid. If men could not travel great distances they could soar to new heights.

Very little was known about the upper atmosphere and scientists were keen to know more and even speculated that by taking measurements of temperature, pressure, wind force and wind speed they would be able to get an instant understanding of the vagaries of the weather. What was not clearly understood was the effect of flying at great heights would have on the aeronauts. At the start of my own aircrew training the other trainees and I were put in a decompression chamber and the oxygen level was steadily decreased. We had all been given simple arithmetic tests to do, which at first seemed childishly simple – but as less oxygen reached our brains we found them more and more difficult – and made stupid mistakes. At the end we understood just why the rules decreed that we should take oxygen whenever flying at more than 10,000 ft. As we know, people do go above that height without oxygen, for example when climbing in the Himalayas, but they do so after a period of acclimatisation. Ballooning does not include that sort of provision – the ascent is rapid and conditions soon become extreme. That in itself makes some of the results reported after flights potentially unreliable –they could get readings as wrong as our answers to simple sums. More importantly, the dangers of high-altitude flying were not really appreciated sometimes with dangerous and even fatal results. Although these real dangers were not properly understood, there was no shortage of imagined dangers – including being hit by meteorite showers that were thought to whiz around at very low levels.

The earliest recorded ascent that claimed to be used for scientific research was made in July 1803 by Etienne-Gaspard Roberts. He had an unlikely career, known as both a lecturer in physics and a stage magician. He used his knowledge of optics to produce special illusions in what he called his Phantasmagoria show. On this first flight, he had a list of experiments he was asked to carry out, prepared by the Acadamie Française and he claimed to have reached an altitude of 23,526 feet. Given that he had only used a rather small hydrogen balloon most experts were convinced that this was quite impossible. At that height, given the greatly reduced air pressure, a great deal of gas would have to have been vented to prevent the balloon bursting. Also, there were two men in the car with a mass of scientific equipment and to reach such a height they would have had to lose virtually all their ballast. With a partially filled envelope and no more ballast to lose, the descent would have been catastrophically fast. Later reports that at altitude he and his companions' hands and even their heads swelled up like balloons seemed, and still seem, absurd.

The French academicians had sponsored Roberts' flight, but their equivalents in Britain showed no interest in following their example. It was left to a wealthy amateur scientist, George Rush, to sponsor a high-level flight in which he would join Charles Green and his large *Nassau* balloon. There were elaborate preparations to ensure that a perfect balance was made between the amount of gas that needed to be in the balloon at take-off and how much ballast needed to be carried and how much jettisoned. The flight took place in September 1838 from Vauxhall Gardens. The crowd expected a spectacle, so the balloon was fully inflated so that it shot skywards and only when it was well above the ground did Green release an appropriate amount of gas and as he rose, ballast was regularly thrown out to gain height. It took just seven minutes to reach 10,000 feet and the balloon continued climbing until eventually their barometer readings indicated that they had reached a final height of 27,126 feet. They had climbed to over five miles above the surface of the earth. Green brought the balloon down safely and unsurprisingly neither of the men recorded swelling hands and heads, but they did report on the bitter cold. It remains a remarkable achievement, and one that very few would contemplate trying to repeat today. Green went on to make more high-level flights this time with John Welsh of the Kew Observatory who was one of the first to develop meteorology into a genuinely scientific discipline. He was able to make more accurate temperature measurements than had been possible before and although they would not be accurate by today's standards, they did show that the upper atmosphere was as variable as that at ground level. Together they reached heights of over 20,000 feet but Green never surpassed the height reached on his first flight.

On one of Green's flights when the air was remarkably clear, one observer was able to follow the entire flight using a telescope.

His name was James Glaisher, who had already established a considerable reputation as a meteorologist. He realised that there were many different aspects of the atmosphere that he could study that were summed up in his own words – 'the determination of the temperature of the air and the hygrometrical condition at different altitudes'. To achieve this he planned flights in which he would take 17 different instruments in order to attempt a dozen different experiments. The first attempt was to be made with Green and his balloon but the attempt was beset with problems. The balloon had simply made too many flights and suffered too much wear and tear. The British Association that was backing the enterprise looked around for an alternative. Their first choice was Thomas Lithgoe and his *Royal Cremorne* balloon but that turned out to be in an even worse condition than *Nassau*. Next, they turned to the experienced aeronaut Henry Coxwell and his balloon *Mars*. Once again, the balloon failed to prove reliable, but Coxwell offered to make a new one with 90,00 cu. ft. capacity that would later be known as *Mammoth*. Together Coxwell and Glaisher were to make 28 ascents, during which the meteorologist was able to do a great deal of important work that resulted in three important scientific papers for the British Association. But none of their flights was as dramatic as the one they made from Wolverhampton on 5 September 1862.

On this occasion everything proceeded well at first, though there were problems with the aspirator that was supposed to provide them with the extra oxygen they would need. But the ascent was rapid and they were soon at a height of around 29,000 feet and the temperature had dropped well below freezing point. The balloon was constantly turning and as a result the valve line had become entangled and Coxwell had to clamber up to the hoop to release it. Below him Glaisher was having difficulty seeing his instruments and then his condition began to get seriously worse, and he described his terrifying ordeal in graphic detail.

'I laid my arm upon the table, possessed of its full vigour, but on being desirous of using it I found it powerless - it must have lost its power momentarily; trying to move the other arm, I found it powerless also. Then I tried to shake myself, and succeeded, but I seemed to have no limbs. In looking at the barometer my head fell over my left shoulder; then I fell backwards, my back resting against the side of the car and my head on its edge. In this position my eyes were directed to Mr Coxwell in the ring.

When I shook my body I seemed to have full power over the muscles of the back, and considerably so over those of the neck, but none over either my arms or my legs. As in the case of the arms, so all muscular power was lost in an instant from my back and neck. I dimly saw Mr Coxwell, and endeavoured to speak, but could not. In an instant intense darkness overcame me, so that my optic nerve lost power suddenly, but I was still conscious, with as active a brain as at the present moment whilst writing this. I thought I'd been seized with asphyxia, and believed I would experience nothing more, as death would come unless we speedily descended.'

Glaisher became vaguely aware of Coxwell talking to him and attempting to revive him. They had begun the descent and gradually he returned to consciousness. Coxwell had almost succumbed as well – if he had then they would certainly have died, but as it was he had been able to bring the balloon back under control. He too had suffered – 'his hands were black' and Glaisher poured brandy over them. It was only after he had recovered that he heard what had happened to Coxwell. His frozen hands had become useless, so he had to wrap his arms round the ring to drop into the car. Once there he needed to pull the line to open the vent, but his hands were unable to grip, and he only managed the essential act that was to save them by grabbing the line with his teeth.

Remarkably, having returned to full consciousness, Glaisher simply carried on taking and recording his scientific measurements until after a rapid descent they finally landed in Shropshire – and Glaisher walked seven miles into Ludlow to get a cart to collect the balloon. Glaisher made his own estimate of the height they had reached as 37,000 feet, though most experts believe that is unlikely – but there is general agreement that they certainly passed the 30,000-foot level. Many men would have abandoned ballooning after such a terrifying and near-fatal experience but they continued with their flights. Glaisher clearly experienced no long-term effects from his ordeal as he remained in good health and continued with his scientific work even after retirement and died at the age of 94.

One would have thought that Glasher's account would act as a warning of the perils of flying too high but the experienced balloonist Gaston Tissandier was sure that he could match Glashier's performance, thanks to a new breathing apparatus. This consisted of a mouthpiece connected by a tube to a bladder containing a mixture of oxygen and air. He had tried it in a decompression chamber where it worked well and he was now ready to test it at altitude. With two scientists, Sivel and Crocé-Spinelli, he set off from a gasworks near Paris in April 1875. Everyone began to feel the effects of altitude as the balloon rose above 20,000 feet, but once they started using the apparatus they felt themselves fully recovered and decided to continue the climb.

As the balloon soared, Tissandier lost consciousness but was revived by the others and urged to throw out ballast, as the balloon was no longer rising but falling far too quickly. Crocé-Spinelli in his eagerness to help jettisoned a very heavy piece of scientific equipment – too heavy as it turned out for once again the balloon began rising and once again Tissandier lost consciousness. He came round to find they were again descending rapidly, but his two companions were laid out, their faces black and blood oozing from nose and mouth. They were dead. Somehow Tissandier managed to make a safe landing.

There were to be a few more high-altitude ascents over the following years in which oxygen cylinders were carried. They were still mainly intended for meteorological research, but once unmanned weather balloons had been developed these risky enterprises came to a stop. It was to be a century later before manned balloons again rose to such heights and then far higher. But if high flying was no longer a major aim of experimental balloonists, there was another problem that exercised their ingenuity: how to make a balloon go where you wanted rather than merely where the wind took it.

CHAPTER SEVEN

Powered Flight

At the very beginning of the age of flight, there were visionaries who were looking for ways of steering balloons and providing a form of propulsion more reliable than the wind. Various ideas had been tried over the years, from oars to sails, but none had been effective. One theorist, however, had clearly understood the problem from the very earliest days. Jean Baptiste Meusnier was a French mathematician, engineer and scientist. As a young man he produced an important mathematical theorem on curved surfaces and he worked with the famous French chemist Antoine Lavoisier in studying hydrogen. Both of these aspects of his work were valuable when he came to consider the nature of balloons and how their performance could be improved. He presented a paper to the French Academy of Sciences in December 1783 on 'the equilibrium of aerostatic machines'. In it he described a device that he called a 'ballonnet'. He was specifically interested in hydrogen balloons and was thinking of ways in which the aeronaut could control his height without releasing the gas. His idea was to have small balloons inside the main envelope that could be filled with air under pressure. He recognised that as the balloon rose into the thinner atmosphere the hydrogen would expand, putting a strain on the fabric. Now instead of having to release the hydrogen he could allow the air to escape from the ballonnet through a valve. Equally, if gas was escaping, air could be pumped in.

In 1784 he took his idea a stage further, designing what could be described as the first dirigible airship. He was well aware from his mathematical work that a spherical balloon was fine for vertical travel but far less satisfactory when it came to moving horizontally. His envelope was in the form of an ellipsoid, roughly 80 metres long, below which was the gondola. This was held in place by lines suspended from a reinforced strip of material running round the balloon. Between the gondola and the main envelope was a wooden structure holding four large propellers. These were to be worked by a crew of men using a rope and pulley system. Steering was via a rudder and elevator. He was almost certainly aware that this was no more than a theoretical concept and that his ideas

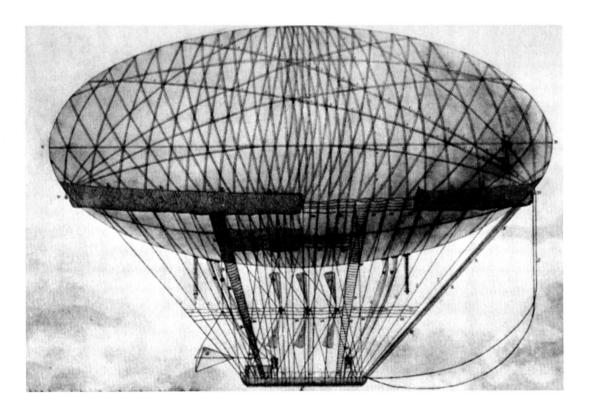

would only really be put into practice when a more efficient power source was found than a gang of sweaty men. He might have gone on to develop more ideas but instead he became an army officer and was killed in 1793, fighting in the French Revolutionary Wars.

Meusnier's ideas were put into practice, in part at least, in 1784 by the Robert brothers and Jacques Charles. They constructed an ellipsoid balloon with a single ballonnet that made its maiden flight on 15 July of that year, with the Roberts and the Duc de Charles on board. Unfortunately, the ballonet had been incorrectly fitted and the aeronauts were unable to release any gas at all, a potentially disastrous situation that was saved, if rather dramatically, by the Duc de Charles slashing a hole in the envelope with his sword. Everyone came down safely, if more rapidly than they would have liked. The principle of the ballonet was sound – it was the workmanship that was at fault and the Robert brothers constructed another ellipsoid balloon in which Cadet Robert made a flight of 150 miles from Paris.

Others worked on the general ideas laid down by Meusnier, including Baron Scott in England, who produced a variation in

Jean-Baptiste Meusnier's design for an airship, which was only impractical because no power source other than human muscles was available.

which two ballonnets were used, one aft and one forward. The idea was that by inflating one and deflating the other, the balance would be altered and offer a form of control that would ensure level flight. It was never put into practice and would almost certainly have had only a very limited effectiveness. The most interesting theory was put forward by one of the great aviation pioneers, Sir George Cayley. He wrote a three-part paper on aerial navigation, published 1809-10, in which he laid down principles on which a dirigible balloon could be built. He suggested that the ideal shape would be 'a very oblong spheroid' that would offer least air resistance and that in order for it retain the shape it should have a longitudinal internal and two lateral braces of light wood. This was the first description of a semi-rigid airship. He then went on to explain how it might be controlled, by adding a very large cruciform rudder for steering, controlling both lateral and vertical movement. This steering idea was to be put into practice a century later by Zeppelin. But Cayley, like Meusnier, realised that without a power source the scheme would have to remain purely theoretical. He abandoned the idea and turned instead to devising heavier than air craft and began building a series of very successful gliders. He returned to the idea of powered balloons, including suggesting a rather strange device using woollen cloth for the envelope. He then proceeded to propose a hydrogen airship that was to be driven along by three tiers of flapping wings, powered by a steam engine 'or any other first mover'. The ship would be 144 yards long and would, he claimed, be able to carry 500 men for one hour and decreasing numbers for longer periods, ending with 50 men for 48 hours, without having to stop to take on fuel and water. The fifty-man version would, he said, be able to cover 960 miles. This extravagant contraption was never put to the test, which is perhaps just as well for Cayley's reputation.

A powered navigable balloon was built in 1850 by a French clockmaker Pierre Julien. It had a long shape of the form recommended by Cayley and was driven by a pair of propellers set to either side. It was demonstrated at the Paris Hippodrome and was an immediate success. It was, of course, only a model – and Julien faced exactly the same problem that had defeated previous inventors – power. Clockwork was not going to be able to drive a full-sized version.

The only likely source of power available at the start of the nineteenth century was the steam engine and it was Henri Giffard who set about adapting it for flight. The main problem to overcome was the weight of the engine itself. In trying to reduce that he looked at one aspect of its working – the substantial pumps required to provide water for the boiler. He realised that these could be dispensed with by using steam pressure to force the water through. The steam injector was to have very little effect on aviation history, but it was soon put into use on railway locomotives, where it became a standard fixture, improved on over the years, for as long as steam locomotives were built.

Giffard had neglected ballooning following his time with his *Eagle* but he was asked to help Dr Le Berrier construct a model steam-powered airship. This was not quite the first use of steam power in the air – John Stringfellow had actually built an aeroplane in 1848 and installed a lightweight steam engine of his own design in 1848 and had gone on to make further models, but again no full-sized version. It was to be Giffard who would take the next major stride forward. He designed what might be considered a genuine airship. The actual dirigible was very similar in appearance to the one designed by Meusnier, an ellipsoid 144 foot long and 40 foot diameter and sharply pointed at both ends. The whole

Henri Giffard's airship, powered by a small steam engine.

envelope was covered by netting to take the weight of the gondola suspended a long way beneath to avoid the chance of any sparks from the furnace igniting the gas. To minimise the risk, the furnace itself was surrounded by a fine wire mesh and the chimney pointed downwards. The engine weighed in at a hefty 350 pounds and was used to drive a three-bladed propeller. There was a rudimentary steering system in the form of a triangular canvas rudder.

It looks an unlikely and ungainly creation, but it took to the skies on a calm Parisian day in September 1852 and puffed away westward at a stately 5 mph to a safe landing 15 miles away. It was not perhaps the most spectacular flight ever made but it was the very first powered flight to be made with a man on board. It was not to be Giffard's last. He used the same craft on several occasions, on one of which he managed to use the rudder to steer round in a complete circle: a task that was only possible because it was a totally calm day. So he could also claim to be the first to fly a powered, steerable balloon. It was a start, but hardly constituted a new, practical form of transport. Giffard recognised that he would need a far larger version in order to carry a more powerful engine.

An early example of an airship powered by an electric motor.

His second version had a capacity of 113,000 cu. ft. and a more streamlined envelope. Unfortunately, just as it was being launched, gas began to escape, one end rose up to the sky and the lines holding the gondola were snapped. Fortunately, it had scarcely had time to clear the ground, so no harm was done. The balloon, however, flew off unencumbered and disappeared into the distance. Giffard at once set about plans for constructing an even bigger version. This would have been an absolute monster, nearly 2,000 ft long with a capacity of almost 8 million cubic feet and designed to carry a thirty-ton engine. Giffard calculated that it should be able to reach a maximum speed of 45 mph. He was convinced this was the crucial next stage that would see powered flying become a regular occurrence. Sadly for him, he could find no backers who shared his optimism and the whole scheme collapsed for lack of funds. His end was sad; plagued by deteriorating eyesight he committed suicide in 1882.

If Giffard had hoped that others would support his venture and perhaps go on to make fresh developments of their own, he was destined to be disappointed. A few tinkered with model making but it was some time before real advances would be made. There was a bizarre experiment in America by Charles F. Ritchel of Pennsylvania. He designed what was, in effect, a small aircraft with a skeletal body, in which the pilot sat and operated a propeller using a hand crank. In order to get it airborne it was suspended from a cylindrical rubber bag filled with gas, the bag having been supplied by Goodyear. The craft itself was built in Ritchel's own workshop. It made its inaugural flight at the 1876 Centennial Exhibition in Philadelphia. It was a novelty that was never developed, but it gave Ritchel the honour of making the first powered flight in the New World.

Other designers and engineers experimented with different power sources. One of these was the gas engine. In 1859 the Belgian engineer Étienne Lenoir began experimenting with electricity and developed a system in which an electric spark could be used to ignite a mixture of gas and air. He adapted a horizontal steam engine to run on the gas-air mixture and produced the first internal combustion engine – and this new gas engine was to prove very successful in industry. The Austrian engineer Paul Haenlein was an experienced balloon pilot who had taken part in the Franco-Prussian War. He decided that the gas engine, which apart from anything else was noted for smooth running, might make a practical alternative to steam power. His device was ingenious. He used a balloon filed with coal gas inside of which was a ballonnet into which air could be pumped. He drew his fuel from the balloon itself and replenished the loss by pumping air into the ballonnet. It was tested in tethered flight but totally failed to live up to expectations. Although the engine was lighter than the steam engine and didn't require either a furnace or extra fuel, this failed to compensate for the fact that the coal gas didn't supply sufficient lift. It did represent, however, another aviation first – the first craft to fly using an internal combustion engine. However, like the other attempts at powered flight, it turned out to be yet another dead end.

The next experiment in mechanical drive systems again turned to electricity, but this time in the shape of the electric motor. Michael Faraday had demonstrated the principle in 1831, when he had shown both how to generate an electric current and also how to use it to create movement, but it had taken some time for a practical motor to be developed. Gaston and Albert Tissandier built a model airship powered by an electric motor that they demonstrated at the Electrical Exhibition in Paris in 1881. It was greeted with such huge enthusiasm that the brothers decided to scale up to a full-sized version. The new craft was 92 feet long, 30 feet in diameter and had a capacity of 37,500 feet. Siemens supplied the electric motor powered by 24 batteries. One unusual feature was that it used a pusher propeller, rather than the pulling or tractor variety that we now associate with aircraft – in the early years of aviation there was considerable debate over which version was the more efficient. The first Tissandier flight started from Auteuil on 8 October 1883 and landed at Croissy-sur-Seine little more than four miles away. A second flight in November went further covering 15½ miles. Neither flight could be called rapid, with an average of just 3 mph The craft suffered from precisely the same problem as the others. The electric motor might have been light but the batteries weighed 17 pounds each, making a total of 408 lbs. Others were to be more successful in using electric power.

The next major step forward was the work of two officers in the French Army, Charles Renard and Arthur Krebs. They were both enthusiastic about the idea of turning balloons into manageable airships, but as serving officers they could not go out and get private finance and the army showed no interest in supporting their experiments. The position changed dramatically when Léon Gametta took over responsibility for reorganising the army after the

Franco-Prussian War. He, of course, had personal experience of the value of flight, having been taken by balloon out of Paris during the war to join the provisional government. He ensured that funds would be made available and personally provided a considerable sum of his own money and the two men began construction of their machine at Chalais Meudon near Paris.

The two engineers were impressed by Haenlein's experimental craft powered by the gas engine and the overall shape of the craft was closely modelled on his design. It was 156 ft long with a maximum diameter of 27 ft and a capacity of 66,000 cubic feet The gondola was very long at 108 ft but only 4½ ft. wide and 6ft. deep. It was constructed on a lightweight bamboo frame, covered with silk and lined with canvas. Renard and Krebs had designed their own batteries that were considerably lighter than those used by the Tissandiers and Krebs designed a multi-polar motor capable of delivering 7½ horse power, built by Renard. This drove a four-bladed wooden tractor propeller that was 23 ft. from blade tip to blade tip mounted at the front of the car. It could be tipped up to avoid damage when landing. Other important features included an efficient rudder and elevator, multiple ballonnets inside the main envelope and a sliding weight that could be used to trim the craft. When everything was assembled, the total weight of the whole power unit was roughly half that of the Tissandier unit. The airship was given a suitably patriotic name – *La France*.

The first flight was memorable and a landmark in aviation history. They set off from Chalais Meudon on the afternoon of 9 August 1884, with the two engineers on board. Once they had reached a height of fifty feet, Renard started the electric motor and they headed off south. The flight was being used not only to test the power unit but also the use of the controls. The original intention seems to have been to head off from base and eventually come down to land at some suitable location, which was the normal practice for such flights. When the rudder was applied, the ship began to turn and the response was so positive that instead of straightening up, Renard kept the rudder held over until the ship had come right round through 180°. So far they had a light following wind, but now they were flying directly into the breeze without difficulty. They arrived back at their base at a height of one thousand feet and by venting gas and using the motor and controls made a triumphant landing right outside the hangar from which they had started. Giffard had managed to fly his craft round in a complete

Dr Karl Woelfort's airship was the first to be powered by a petrol engine and led the way to future developments.

circle, but that had been on a totally calm day. Now, for the very first time, a craft had been developed that really could be accurately controlled and could land its crew and passengers at the place of their choice. The ambition that had driven so many aeronauts over the years – the desire to make their craft go in whichever direction they chose – had finally been realised.

There were to be more flights that year, the majority of which were able to land back where they started. A few changes were made – the original motor was replaced by the more efficient Gramme electric motor – the machine that was to be an important source of power for many nineteenth century industries. *La France* was an undoubted success, able to travel at a respectable average speed of 4 mph but it had its limitations. It was quite capable of travelling against light winds, but if wind speeds increased there was simply not enough power available. It was the problem that beset all these aeronauts struggling to develop powered flight. They had still not found a really satisfactory solution to the difficulties caused by the poor power to weight ratio of their machines. To get more power required a bigger motor and more batteries and the extra weight then required far greater lifting power to get them off the ground. Renard and Krebs had demonstrated that there was a future for airships – but that future would depend still on finding a better, lighter power source.

Krebs was to go on to have a distinguished career, working in very different fields – designing France's first submarine and later applying his ingenuity to improving automobile design, and it was in the realm of road transport that the breakthrough appeared that was to launch the age of the airship. There were several innovations that combined to make progress possible. N.A. Otto had improved the efficiency of the two-stroke gas engine by devising the four-stroke version – compression, ignition, expansion, exhaust. Gottlieb Daimler had adapted the idea but instead of gas used petrol as the fuel. He used the new, small efficient engine to produce the world's first motorbike, powered by an internal combustion engine. In the meantime. new processes had been developed simultaneously in France and America for the production of aluminium. The combination of light, strong metal and efficient engine was exactly what was required to turn airships from experimental craft to commercial flying machines.

To follow the account of what happened next, we have to step back a little in time to look at the exploits of two German aeronauts. Dr Karl Woelfert began his career as a minister in a church at Leipzig but seems not to have found the vocation much to his liking. He then became involved in a succession of mainly unsuccessful commercial ventures that lost rather more money than they gained. He had developed an interest in ballooning and decided to become a full-time aeronaut. His first public ascents were much like those of others at that period, taking off from various pleasure gardens in front of a paying crowd. His craft, however, was very different, being very elongated, earning it the nickname 'the cucumber'. In 1882 he met a verderer from Saxony called Baumgarten who had devised a form of powered balloon. He had already built a small airship that used a hand-operated propeller for lift but depended for forward motion on a type of glider wing. Woelfert suggested dumping the gliders and replacing them with a second propeller.

Together they built a larger craft, with three compartments, in each of which a man could sit to work one of the three propellers that were now used.

The first flight ended with the airship rearing up, nose first, before crashing to the ground. Both men had now joined the Berlin Aeronautical Society and the Society, in spite of this unpromising start, was sufficiently interested in these experiments to provide funds for a second craft to be built. The result was even worse – this time the airship crashed at the Charlottenberg Gardens and Baumgarten died from his injuries. Woelfert, however, continued with his experiments He used a small balloon, with two hand-operated propellers, one for lift and one for forward motion. He made a number of test flights, but inevitably it was clear that development was impossible without a non-human power source. However, the flights aroused some public interest and were reported in the local press, *Leipziger Illustrierte Zeitung*. The account was read by Daimler in Stuttgart and he was at once intrigued by the notion of combining his petrol engine with Woelfert's navigable balloon and wrote to the inventor suggesting he should come to discuss ideas at his workshop at Cannstatt.

Woelfort arrived with his tiny balloon and a 2 hp petrol engine was fitted into the car. On 12 August 1888, everything was ready for a test flight. Woelfort himself was too weighty to make the pioneering ascent so the job went to one of the lightest of Daimler's mechanics, who we simply know as Michaël. It was a hazardous business as the car was slung right below the envelope and the engine relied on an ignition system kept going by a burner using vaporised petrol from a pressure cylinder. During the flight the movement of air from the propeller kept blowing out the pilot light, which then had to be relit using a candle. The young man probably did not realise just how dangerous his situation was, for even the smallest spark from the burner or the candle could have turned the balloon into a fireball. In the event, all went well and he landed safely. There were to be two more flights before Daimler withdrew from the enterprise. He must have considered the rival calls on his time; should he concentrate on the experimental airship or give all his attention to developing the engine for use on the road? He decided, probably wisely, as far as the potential market was concerned, on the latter course.

Woelfert was now faced with a major problem, for he was well aware that future development would depend as much on improvements in engine design as on any variations in the airship itself. He did manage to fund a second craft that was to be powered by a more powerful, two-cylinder 6 h.p. Daimler engine and he took this new version to the Berlin Trade Fair of 1896. Even though it was only on static display it attracted a great deal of attention and several businessmen offered to fund future developments. Woelfert was aware that if only he could demonstrate the craft in flight there would be a far better chance of getting serious investment and then he received a surprising offer of help. Kaiser Wilhelm II visited the show, was impressed and offered the inventor the use of the Prussian Balloon Corps airfield at Templehof, a site that was later to become the city's airport.

The day chosen for the flight was 12 June and watched by a considerable crowd, including many representatives of European countries, the craft took off with Woelfertt and an engineer, Robert Knabe. There were various reports of what happened next, but everyone agreed that there seemed to be difficulty in keeping the craft flying a steady course, and some reported seeing damage to the rudder. Nevertheless, it cleared the field and flew out across the city, levelling out at about 3,000 feet. Down below, people came out into the streets and their gardens to watch the spectacle, but awe-struck admiration turned in an instant to pure horror. Two flames were seen to leap from the engine, followed shortly afterwards by a loud explosion and in an instant the whole ship

Le Jaune on display in the Galerie des Machines in Paris.

was ablaze and crashing to earth as a fireball. The two men on board had no chance of surviving such a complete disaster.

It is always easy with hindsight to see why things had gone so badly wrong, The first error was having the engine fitted so close to the envelope: had the car been suspended lower down the whole ship would not have been set ablaze. Things might also have been different had Daimler still been involved, since by this time he had invented an improved ignition system that did not involve a naked flame. Such a very public disaster might well have marked an end to this line of development, but others had already been working on similar plans.

David Schwartz was born in Hungary, then part of the Austrian Empire and worked as a timber merchant. This involved long days and dreary nights working out in the forest, and his wife Melanie sent him books to keep him amused. One of these gave details of new ideas in airship design, and Schwartz was so fascinated he decided to build an airship himself. He took his plans to the war minister of the Austro-Hungarian Empire who said he was interested but not to the point where he was prepared to authorise his department to put money into the venture. The Russian military attaché, however, took a much more positive view and suggested to Schwartz that he should come to St. Petersburg. Once there he designed an aluminium framed airship, but when it was inflated the whole structure collapsed. A Russian engineer suggested that he should include separate gas bags and ballonnets to remove the stresses. In this way, the pressure would only act on the individual containers, and not on the outer skin. The original plan called for a four-cylinder engine rated at 10 horse power as the driving force but it seems uncertain just how far the project went as Schwartz left Russia in something of a hurry.

In 1894, he made contact with the industrialist Carl Berg, and together they put forward a new proposal, this time to the Royal Prussian Government. Work got under way the following year but everything came to a temporary halt when Schwartz died in 1895. However, Melanie Schwartz, whose choice of reading matter had set the whole thing in motion, took over her husband's role. The airship was 156 feet long, with an elliptical cross section – 39 feet wide and 46 feet high, with a capacity of 130,000 cubic feet. It looked rather like an oversized pencil, with a round body, pointed nose and flat stern. Power was to be supplied once again by a Daimler engine, this time a twin-cylinder 12 horse power version. This was to work three aluminium tractor propellers, one to each side of the car and the third at the stern. Unlike the ill-fated Woelfert design the car was suspended some way below the balloon.

Once again, the maiden flight was to take off from Templehof. It was successfully inflated on 2 November 1897 and was made ready for the flight the next morning. Conditions were not ideal with a stiff breeze blowing at ground level. Somewhat surprisingly, controls were in the hands of a single pilot, whose identity is uncertain; either the chief engineer on the project or an officer from the Balloon Corps. The latter might seem the more likely, as only an experienced aeronaut could be expected to handle such a craft single-handed. On the other hand, an experienced aeronaut might well have seen that the task was well-nigh impossible in the circumstances. However, the flight was destined to be a short one. The whole ship had only reached a height of 80 feet when the belt driving the three propellers snapped. The pilot, not surprisingly, panicked and promptly vented gas, but far too quickly. The machine plummeted to the ground and the pilot was just able to jump clear before the whole thing collapsed on top of him.

Other innovators were considering the possibilities of both airships and the newly developed motor vehicles. Alberto Santon-Dumont was a wealthy Brazilian, whose family owned extensive coffee plantations. He arrived in Paris in 1897 as a young man still in his twenties, eager to sample everything the new life in Europe had to offer. He bought the very latest things, including a De Dion-Bouton motorised tricycle that had only been put on the market that year – at an exorbitantly high price. It was powered by a 211cc engine producing just 1.5 horse power, but that was quite sufficient as the engine itself was lightweight and the whole machine weighed just 80 kilograms. At much the same time he took his first flight in a balloon and was enchanted by the experience. He was a man fascinated by machinery – as a child he had learned to drive a steam tractor. He was also an avid reader of the works of Jules Verne and was enthralled by his visions of future transport systems. All these elements now came together; he recognised that the light tricycle engine could be adapted to powering a balloon and that would enable him to fulfil his childhood dreams of flying. Just as importantly, he had quite enough money of his own to make those dreams a reality.

Santos-Dumont was very ready to recognise the debt he owed to earlier aeronauts, particularly Giffard and he made use of many of that pioneer's design ideas in constructing his own craft that was simply called *Dirigible No.1*. The first flight was planned for 18 September 1898 from the Jardin d'Acclamitation in Paris's zoological gardens. He planned to take off into the wind but was assured by the several 'experts' gathered for the occasion that this would be absolute folly and would end in disaster. He took their advice, had the ship turned, climbed into the gondola and set off – and was promptly carried by the wind into a stand of trees. The ship was retrieved, necessary repairs carried out and two days later he was ready to go again. This time, Santon-Dumont followed his own instincts and took off into the wind and soared away. Once he had reached altitude, he turned the ship and flew back over the cheering crowd, acknowledging the applause by raising his shiny top hat. He was able to demonstrate the ship's manageability by successfully steering a figure of eight course over the Parisian suburbs. It seemed that he had made the perfect maiden flight but once he began to descend for a landing everything started to go wrong.

He had risen to around 1300 feet and had vented a great amount of gas. Now as he began to come down, the air pumps were unable to pump in enough air to compensate. Not only was he coming down rather too rapidly but the envelope was beginning to collapse in the middle. Disaster seemed inevitable, but he spotted a group of boys playing a field, threw down the trail rope and shouted to them to grab hold of it and run as fast as they could against the wind. The youngsters must have thought this was a great adventure and set off with all the speed they could manage. Progress was slowed, the ship dragged along the ground but landed safely.

Santon-Dumont went on to build more dirigibles and make more flights. His greatest achievement came on 19 October 1901. Henry Deutsch de la Meurthe was a very wealthy industrialist and flying enthusiast, a member of the Paris Aero Club. He offered a prize of 100, 000 francs, a considerable sum of money, for anyone who could take off from the club's field at St. Cloud, fly round the Eiffel Tower, and land back at the field in under half an hour. Santon-Dumont took up the challenge for the pure excitement of the venture: he certainly didn't need the money. He succeeded on his sixth attempt and calculated that he had achieved an average speed of 25 kilometres per hour (15½ mph) the fastest yet achieved by any airship.

He was a man with a flair for the dramatic and made regular trips round Paris in a small motorised balloon of just 7,700 cubic feet capacity. On one occasion he flew right down the Champs Elysée, sailing regally past the Arc de Triomphe and even more remarkably he realised that he was close to his favourite café and simply dropped down outside the door and parked, much as a modern traveller might park a car. He sat and enjoyed his drink and then set off again.

Santon-Dumont became a highly skilled pilot and did a great deal to popularise flight. Unfortunately, not everyone who decided it would be fun to follow his example was as proficient. When Augusto Severo built a dirigible and set out to fly it with his mechanic in 1894, the ascent was too rapid. He threw out ballast instead of venting, the craft shot up rapidly, the pressure inside the envelope increased until it burst and the craft fell to the earth in flames, killing both men. Shortly afterwards there was another disaster when, in October, Paul Morin's airship ran into strong winds, went out of control and crashed, again killing those on board. The art and science of flying were still not fully understood but in spite of several tragedies, there were always those ready to move on and try to make improvements. The years at the beginning of the twentieth century saw the first flight of a dirigible whose size and performance surpassed anything that had gone before.

The airship was built for the brothers Paul and Pierre Lebaudy, who owned a large sugar refinery, and was designed for them by their chief engineer at the works, Henri Julliot. It was 187 foot long and had a capacity of 90,000 cubic feet. The propellers were mounted either side of the gondola and were powered by a 35 horse power Daimler engine. On its very first flight in November 1903 it achieved a speed of 25 mph and was able to climb to 3,000 feet without venting gas it proved admirably manoeuvrable. Officially named simply *Lebaudy I*, its rather bright yellow colour meant that popularly it was always known as *Le Jaune*. It made a number of successful flights and Parisians had a chance to see it close up when it was displayed for a week in the Galerie des Machines built for the 1889 Paris Exposition, near the Champ de Mars. There was one forced landing that caused considerable damage that resulted in it being totally rebuilt. This was the craft that really showed that the airship could be a real and useful form of transport, a fact emphasised in 1905 when *Lebaudy II* made a journey of 128 miles in six and a half hours. The brothers built more airships and found customers in several countries, while *Lebaudy II* itself was later bought by the French Army. Flying was about to enter a new phase when it would no longer be just available to a few aeronauts and their friends but would be opened up to the public at large – or at least that portion of the public who could pay for the privilege of being taken to their destination by air.

CHAPTER EIGHT

The Zeppelin

If Montgolfier is the one name most closely associated with the early years of ballooning, then, when we come to consider airships, the equivalent must be Zeppelin. The name comes from a corruption of the word 'czapla', meaning stork, and was given to an area of land near the Baltic. By the thirteenth century, the first settlement to be named Zepelin was recorded, and the name was also given to the family that owned the land. It was they who added the extra 'p' to the name and in 1834 Graf Friedrich von Zeppelin moved to Konstanz near Lake Constance. He married a wealthy French woman and they had three children. The eldest boy, Ferdinand Graf von Zeppelin, was born in 1838 and was educated by a tutor until he was sent to a secondary school that specialised in science teaching, after which he entered a military academy near Stuttgart. He left college at the age of twenty and became a junior officer in an infantry regiment. The rather easy life of a peacetime officer changed abruptly when war broke out between the Austrian-Hungarian Empire and France over Piedmont, a war that was

A Zeppelin in its floating hangar on Lake Constance.

conducted on the German side with what von Zeppelin regarded as considerable incompetence. When he was mobilised, he opted to join the engineering corps, a decision that caused considerable surprise and not a little dismay to his family, as engineering was not considered a suitable occupation for an aristocrat. As a result of his experiences, he became convinced that the German Army was hopelessly out of date and was determined to investigate a different form of organisation that was being practised in America. After the war, he applied for permission to go there.

In the event, he was given a year's leave, and thanks to his aristocratic connections he was able to depart for America bearing the magnificent title: Count Zeppelin, Chargé des Affaires de Son Majestie le Roi de Würtemberg. He arrived in May 1863 in the middle of the Civil War and managed to join the Army of the Potomac to see the war at close quarters – and was actually caught up in fierce fighting. After that experience he set off to travel and see more of the country. He eventually reached St. Paul in Minnesota where he met John H. Steiner who had served with Thaddeus Lowe in the Federal Balloon Corps. He was invited to join him on a flight and the experience delighted him and kindled an interest in the whole concept of lighter than air flight.

Von Zeppelin returned to his army career in time to take a minor part in the Franco-Prussian War, where once again he was made aware of the potential for the development of balloons when the French used them to get messages out from the besieged city of Paris. He was also aware that several of these balloons had landed in German hands, simply because they could not be steered but were blown off their intended course. At about the same time he came across a book written in 1870 by Heinrich von Stephan, the postmaster of the North German Confederation, in which he put forward his ideas for a regular postal service by balloon. By now von Zeppelin had become convinced that the future lay with dirigibles, and a riding accident in 1874 was bad enough to see him having to make a lengthy stay in hospital. But this misfortune gave him time to think about the best possible design for a steerable balloon.

Von Zeppelin's army career was undemanding in peacetime, which gave him ample opportunity to keep up with the many advances being made with lighter than air machines. He was particularly impressed by the work of Renaud in France and he began to think seriously about the military use of airships. Germany had formed its first Balloon Corps in 1884, with very few men, little funding and no balloon. The only way they could gain actual flying experience was by borrowing one from a female acrobat who used it for public displays on Sundays. It was not a very encouraging situation, but that did not prevent von Zeppelin from putting forward his ambitious ideas in a written report to the king of Würtemberg in 1887. He argued the case for a military airship but explained that to be useful it would have to be able to carry a large number of men, weapons and ammunition and be capable of extended flights, lasting as long as twenty four hours. He suggested that the only way this would be possible would be to use a very large hydrogen balloon to provide the necessary lift and in order for it to retain its shape in flight it would need a rigid internal structure. This was a proposal for future development, not a fully worked out plan, for von Zeppelin still had many elements of the design to work out before such a craft could be constructed and would be capable of the task he had described. There were several factors that he had not yet considered in any sort of detail. He was uncertain about the ideal shape for the craft and was aware, as other pioneers had been, that as yet no one had found a satisfactory power source. Two other problems exercised him: could he control the height of the craft without either jettisoning ballast to rise or venting gas to descend and how would it be steered. He knew what he would like to achieve but was still a very long way from doing so.

By 1890, von Zeppelin had reached the peak of his army career after being given the command of a cavalry brigade at which point he unexpectedly resigned. For a long time, he had found the rigid thinking of the German high command to be a barrier to new ideas and to any sort of progress, and he was fairly certain that they would be very unlikely to back his ideas for airships. It must have been frustrating for him to follow the advances being made in other parts of Europe, while his own plans remained on paper. At much the same time Otto Lilienthal had started experimenting with heavier than air craft. He made a number of successful flights in a machine that looks rather more like a modern hang glider than a modern conventional glider. To von Zeppelin this was a further stimulus to his own ideas. He felt that the Lilienthal idea had a long way to go before it could become a practical, powered machine and that in the meantime there was a place in the world for a successful airship. He decided it was time to put his ideas into practice.

Von Zeppelin was sufficiently well versed in engineering and science to appreciate that if he was to succeed in the absence of established guidelines he would have to develop a research programme. To help him he employed an engineer called Theodor Kober who had considerable experience, having worked in the balloon factory at Augsburg where the Woelfert airship, described in the previous chapter, had been constructed. They set out on a systematic series of trials, testing various propeller designs by mounting them on boats with different engines. They built models to discover the best possible shape for the airship body and considered how to devise a gondola that would remain in perfect balance. One idea was to have three separate sections, one for the pilot and crew, one for the power unit and a third for passengers. They also began to do costings and realised that though costs could be reduced if the airship went into production, the expense of building and testing the prototype could be as much as a million marks, the equivalent of some 6 million euros today. Von Zeppelin was rich but not that rich. He appealed unsuccessfully for government funds and when that proved to be hopeless, applied directly to the emperor, suggesting that a commission should be set up to test whether or not his plans were worth pursuing. The Emperor agreed and the commission was duly appointed with the distinguished scientist Hermann von Helmholtz at its head. Much to von Zeppelin's disappointment the committee decided the airship was not worth funding.

It was now clear that if anything was to be done, then von Zeppelin would have to look to other sources for investment. He set about raising support and this time he was successful in gaining the approval of the Society of German Engineers. They offered very real practical help in the form of a team of expert engineers to help with the design stage. In August 1898 he was able to take out a patent for an airship that consisted of three sections: the first pointed part supported the power unit housed in a gondola; the middle, cylindrical section carried a second gondola, intended for passengers, and the pointed rear section had the third gondola for freight. All sections were based on an aluminium frame. Now that the plans had been given the official seal of approval by Germany's most prestigious engineering organisation, von Zeppelin was able to raise around 800,000 marks, quite enough to begin the serious business of construction.

Once the essential preparatory tests had been completed, the time had arrived to look for a construction site. The chosen site was Friedrichshafen by Lake Constance and by 1898 a combined workshop and hangar had been completed and the actual work of construction could begin. The airship was taken out of its hangar onto a floating platform on the lake on 2 July 1900. Named simply *Luftschiff Zeppelin No.1 – Airship Zeppelin No. 1 –* a name soon abbreviated to the more concise *LZ1*, it looked very impressive. Inside the airship, the interior was divided into seventeen compartments holding 400,000 cubic feet of hydrogen. Beneath it were two gondolas, each holding a 15 horse power Daimler engine. The ship rose to a height of a little over 1,000 feet covering a total distance of 8 miles. Experienced observers could see from the start that it was following a distinctly wobbly and erratic course: the two small rudders were ineffective, and the sliding weights designed to correct the trim were not working. It had flown, landed safely, but was hardly a resounding success. It was now literally a case of 'back to the drawing board'.

Modifications to the steering mechanism were made and for the second flight the Frankfurt newspaper sent along a young economics reporter, Hugo Eckener, to write an account of the flight. He was not very enthusiastic, but as well as being an economist he was also a keen sailor and told von Zeppelin that the craft was too slow to make headway against anything other than a light breeze. On the third trial flight Eckener was proved to be right and there

Zeppelin *LZ2* preparing to set off from Lake Constance.

was no avoiding the dismal fact that *LZ1* was a failure and there was no longer enough cash left in the coffers to pay for further development. The company was wound up and von Zeppelin was more or less back where he started. Once again, he looked for official support by writing to Kaiser Wilhelm II, but never even received a reply. He then decided to appeal to the public at large through the press. That brought in some money, a lottery brought in more and finally there was a significant contribution from an aluminium manufacturer, Berg, who had the foresight to see what success would mean in terms of future orders for the metal. Work got under way from a new site donated by the city of Friedrichschafen near the lake.

The really important difference in the design was the choice of engine. *LZ2* was to be powered by a pair of 85 horse power engines, a huge increase over the power available for *LZ1*. There seemed to be nothing fundamentally wrong with the design, but the test flights were plagued with misfortune. On the first outing on 30 November 1903, the forward engine suddenly cut out, the stern collapsed into the water, damaging the rudder, but the craft rose again into the air and set off across the lake, totally out of control. However, safety precautions had been taken and a fast launch was already standing by and it shot off after the airship and the boat crew managed to grasp the trail rope and save the situation. A second flight on 17 January 1904 appeared to be going rather better. The craft took off and reached a height of over 1500 feet at a respectable speed of 35 mph Then, once again, the forward engine died and the crew were unable to restart it. They were forced to make an emergency landing, during which the stern got caught up in the branches of a tree. It was decided to secure it for the night and return the next day to arrange to get the airship back to base. But in the night a violent storm broke out, reducing the whole fabric to a tattered wreck. Instead of being brought safely back for repair, there was nothing to be done except break it into fragments and try to see if anything could be salvaged from the wreckage.

Needless to say, the fiasco resulted in a total lack of public support for the whole project. But Graf von Zeppelin was not a man to give up without a fight. He used every last mark that he had, borrowed where he could and scraped together enough funds to embark on *LZ3* that was very similar to the second airship. It was after all not a design fault that had caused the problems, but simply an engine failure on both occasions. The new ship made her maiden flight on

9 October 1906 and no doubt to von Zeppelin's immense relief was a triumph. The craft covered a distance of sixty miles at an average speed of 30 mph and did the same again the next day. She went on to make many more flights and established a new endurance record in 1907 by staying airborne for 8 hours. The name 'Zeppelin' was no longer a joke. People began to take it seriously. The Airship Commission made a grant of 500,000 marks for future development, part of which was used to build a larger floating hangar. The Army showed an interest and indicated that they would consider buying an airship provided it met their exacting specifications. Perhaps they remembered von Zeppelin's earlier claim that to be useful it must be able to stay airborne for 24 hours – and that is what they now demanded with a further condition that it must be able to fly non-stop for a thousand kilometres. This was way beyond anything *LZ3* could achieve, so a fourth model was now needed.

LZ4 was slightly bigger than her predecessor, 446 ft long as against 413 ft. but the same diameter of 38ft 6in. The main difference was with the engines, each rated at 105 horse power. The maiden flight on twentieth June 1908 went well and on her third flight over Switzerland she covered almost 200 miles in 12 hours. The Zeppelin received a great publicity boost in July when the king and queen of Würtemberg came aboard for a short flight. Things were going so well that it was decided to make an attempt at the very first 24-hour flight. The intention was to take off from the home base on Lake Constance and then fly over Switzerland as far as Mainz, perform a celebratory circuit over the city and then return via the same route. Flight details were sent to the major towns along the route so that people could come out and watch the spectacle of an airship passing over their heads. On 4 August, *LZ4* was towed from the hangar and the crew and passengers, eleven in all, were taken out by launch. Von Zeppelin himself was to take charge.

At 7 o'clock on a bright, clear morning the craft rose into the air and set off on the epic flight. At first all went well as they set off to follow the course of the Rhine. At 9.30 a.m. they flew over Berne where crowds had come into the streets to wave and cheer. They pressed on – Strasbourg at 12.30, Darmstadt at 4.30 and were heading for the turning point when it became clear that there was a problem. The oil pressure in the forward engine was falling and the temperature rising. Von Zeppelin decided it was not worth risking a complete engine failure and diverted for a landing near Oppenheim. Fortunately, the problem did not appear to be very serious, repairs were made and they took off again. Their optimism was short lived as the same engine again showed signs of causing trouble and it seemed that during the earlier incident a connecting rod bearing had burnt out. Once again, they had to come down, this time near Stuttgart. Von Zeppelin went off to have breakfast at an inn and waited for word to arrive that everything was ready for the final part of the trip. Inevitably a large crowd had gathered, and police and troops had been called in to keep them from getting too close to avoid damaging the craft. Then the wind started to get up and the troops were called on to hang on to the mooring ropes. No one could foresee any real problem, but then apparently a sudden unexpectedly strong gust caught the ship broadside end, sending it rearing into the air where it hit a group of trees and exploded into a mass of flames. Once again, a flight designed to show off the viability of the airship had ended in total disaster.

It is difficult to imagine how von Zeppelin must have thought at this time. He was now seventy years old and it must have seemed that all his dreams had quite literally gone up in flames and many men would simply have given up and retired from the fray. That was never going to be his way of doing things. He at once began planning the next airship and he had an enthusiast to help sway public opinion. Hugo Eckerman, who had not been very enthusiastic when watching the flight of *LZ1*, now took on the part time role of public relations officer and sent out bulletins to all the main newspapers of the country with the message that it was not a personal reputation that was at stake, but national pride. It was up to all patriotic Germans to help the fatherland lead the world in conquering the air. The scheme was a spectacular success. Money poured in and a new company, the Zeppelin Foundation for the Promotion of Aerial Navigation, was set up to handle finance, while the Zeppelin Airship Company concentrated on design and construction. Eckerman now became a full-time member of the company and was to go on to get a pilot's licence and eventually an appointment as director of flying operations.

LZ5 was even bigger than number 4 and the engine power had been increased to 200 horse power. Once again it was decided to make a spectacular long-distance flight, this time to Berlin and then circle the royal palace at nearby Potsdam before returning to Freidrichschafen. Calculations suggested that there was enough fuel on board for the round trip, but that was based on the assumption that there would be good conditions all the way. Instead, the wind got up, the airship had to use more power to make progress against it and it was clear that there was no possibility of achieving the flight. This time the aborted trip had nothing to do with any mechanical failure but rather the lack of any reliable meteorological service to give accurate weather forecasts. At least on this occasion the ship returned safely and was accepted by the army and renamed Z2. She was not destined for a long military career, having been heavily damaged on a landing and then, like earlier ships, wrecked by high winds. The army decided that they could do a better job of airship design themselves and began working on a non-rigid craft, leaving von Zeppelin to carry on without them.

From the very first, von Zeppelin had seen the airship's main role as being military, hardly surprising given his own long career in the army. By this time the company had a new business manager, Coleman, who was related to the aluminium manufacturer Berg. He and Eckerman persuaded von Zeppelin that as there were no orders from the army, nor it seemed likely to be any in the immediate future, he should consider turning the airships over to a new role, carrying fee paying passengers. In 1909 the passenger transport company was formed *Deutsche Luftschiffharts-Aktien-Gessellschaft* – German Airship Transport Company – usually and more conveniently simply known as DELAG. It was set up with the active participication of the major cities of Germany, who at once began preparing airfields and hangars. It was the world's first commercial airline.

A new airship was promptly ordered for the pioneering service and the number was replaced by a suitably patriotic name *Deutschland*. On 22 June, with 32 passengers on board, there was a two-and-a-half-hour trouble-free flight to Dusseldorf. On the sixth flight, once again the elements took control, and buffeted by a strong headwind the craft was forced into a landing in a forest, fortunately without any loss of life. *Deutschland II* was the next victim. A flight had been scheduled with a number of important guests on board, and rather than disappoint them the decision was taken to go ahead, in spite of a rather blustery wind. As the vessel was being manoeuvred out of the hangar, a gust caught the forward portion and slammed it into the side of the door, causing considerable damage. It was then that Eckener, who was by now in charge of operations, made a rule that no more flights should be attempted in bad weather, and more importantly began the business of setting up a meteorological service to keep them informed of what weather they might expect.

More and more airships were being brought into service. The *Schwaben* began her flying career in July 1911 and had completed 218 flights, carrying a total of 1,553 passengers before an all too familiar fate overtook her. She had just landed at Dusseldorf on 28 June 1912 and passengers and crew had just disembarked, when she was caught by a violent storm that quite literally shook the airship to pieces. Earlier that same year *LZ11 – Viktoria Luize –* was completed and enjoyed a successful career: in just over a year and a half after her launch the airship was carrying her 8000th passenger. More craft came into service and by the start of the First World War DELAG they had notched up over 100,000 air miles and carried over 10,000 passengers.

Von Zeppelin was always on the lookout for new ways of using his airships and one particularly attractive idea was Arctic exploration. He was convinced that an airship could succeed where the André balloon expedition had failed. He organised the Zeppelin Arctic expedition that set off in 1910 and eventually made a base at Spitzbergen. Von Zeppelin himself, though now over seventy, took a very active role, ascending in a balloon to survey

A Zeppelin gondola.

the landscape and travelling long distances by dog sledge, with the idea of discovering whether it would be feasible for an airship to make a safe landing in the frozen wilderness. No expedition actually materialised from this survey, but it did attract a great deal of publicity. As a direct result, the German Navy decided to step in where the Army had chosen not to tread.

Admiral Tirpitz was determined to make the German navy as powerful as any in the world – and, if possible, outdo all others. One area under consideration was the use of airships for reconnaissance. He had despatched an officer to watch the trial flights of *LZ3* and although he was given a favourable report, he was unconvinced that the craft could be developed to the point where it could make long voyages out over the North Sea in all weather conditions: a view that was certainly correct as far as peformance at that time was concerned. By 1910 the idea was again under serious consideration, but the leading naval architect of the day, Felix Pietzker, gave his opinion that to be useful an airship should be capable of working against a headwind of 50 knots. He gave Tirpitz his considered opinion of what such a craft would be like – it would be long and sleek, with a capacity of over a million cubic feet and would need to be powered by six 140 horse power engines. When the idea was put to the Zeppelin engineers, they reported back that such a craft would be far beyond current capabilities. But the Kaiser had been struck by the idea of the Arctic airship expedition as being a great boost to German international standing and began pressing the navy to order a ship. Tirpitz had little choice other than to agree, and in 1912 they took delivery of the first naval airship *L1*.

The airship was bigger than the ones currently being built for DELAG with a capacity of almost 800,000 cu. ft., 518ft long and 48ft 6in. diameter and was ready for delivery in October 1912. Von Zeppelin took personal control of the operation, flying out over the North Sea to the Danish coast and then turning for Berlin. The craft had been in the air for over 30 hours and covered more than a thousand miles. It was by far the most impressive flight yet made by a Zeppelin. Meanwhile the Navy had been building an airship base at Nordholz near the North Sea coast in Lower Saxony. At the same time, they were beginning to train crews. Tirpitz was sufficiently convinced to set up a five-year development programme and began ordering more airships. There were successful exercises during which *L1* shadowed the fleet and was able to radio reports of 'enemy' shipping movements. On 14 August she took off again on another training exercise with a crew of twenty officers and men on board. At first all went well, but an hour and a half into the flight, cruising off the coast of Heligoland, the wireless operator received warning of an approaching storm. The captain at once decided to abandon the exercise and head for home, but they were too late. The storm overtook them and the ship was sent plummeting into the waves. There were no survivors. Just two months later *L2* was also undergoing trial flights. On the morning of 17 October she took off with 28 people on board, which consisted of the crew of fifteen and a number of observers, including Felix Pietzker who had advised Tirpitz in the early days. The craft rose rapidly, but after making one circuit of the field, spectators saw a burst of flame from one of the engines. Seconds later, the whole ship was ablaze and falling to the ground. Soldiers rushed to the scene, but the fierce heat made it impossible to do anything to save the men on board. Two were pulled out alive but so severely burned that they died within hours. In spite of these terrible tragedies in which virtually the whole of the experienced aircrew had been killed, Tirpitz pushed ahead with the development of airships that were to play a vital role when war broke out in 1914.

The Zeppelins undoubtedly dominated the decade leading up to the war, but they did not have the field entirely to themselves. There were some who took a different view on designs. August von Parseval, like von Zeppelin, came from a military background. He favoured non-rigid airships. They had the advantage of being lighter since there was no internal metal frame and that meant they were able to carry heavier loads. In general, however, they were slower than the Zeppelins and attempts to make ever bigger versions were thwarted by the inability to keep the shape of the envelope intact at speed. They were notable, however, for a demonstration of things to come: in1909 they were used to carry out a simulated raid on a military fort. In spite of this early indication that the airships could be actively used in wartime, a number were built under licence by Vickers in Britain and supplied to the Royal Navy, soon to be facing the German fleet in battle.

The main rival to the Zeppelins came not from the military this time, but from the academic world. Johann Schütte was Professor of Naval Architecture at Danzig University who set up a company, Schütte-Lanz. He designed rigid airships, but instead of aluminium used laminated plywood. As a naval architect he was very conscious of how important the shape of a hull was in moving efficiently through water and he brought the same expertise to his design of airships that were noticeably more streamlined and sleek than the Zeppelins. He also introduced a feature that must have been welcomed by the crew: the pilot's gondola was completely enclosed. Rather like early steam locomotive engineers who believed providing a cab for their drivers would make things too comfortable and they might lose concentration, so von Zeppelin believed his pilots should have the wind in their faces. The first version *SL1* was powered by a pair of motors providing a top speed of 38 mph but the second version had four engines and was considered highly successful. When war broke out the company was taken over by the government and merged with Zeppelin.

Germany was the most important centre for development of airships during the opening years of the twentieth century, but it was not alone. In the next chapter we shall look at what the rest of the world was doing.

CHAPTER NINE

Spreading the Word

The French had led the way in developing powered airships and the movement had been carried forward to produce the first commercial airships, the Zeppelins. Britain, a country that in the nineteenth century had led the world in innovation and manufacture, was notably slow in joining the development programme. As in Germany, the first thoughts of would-be airship designers turned to their military use. The military balloons had proved their value, especially in the Boer Wars, and the head of the balloon division, Colonel James Templer, was keen to develop an airship. He had a distinguished record with the military balloon group, though it nearly came to an abrupt end in 1888, when he was arrested and charged with sending secrets about Britain's balloons to the Italian government. The charge was proved to be without any foundation and his military career continued with no further setbacks. His efforts to persuade the War Office to fund an airship project were rejected time after time but in 1902 he was finally given permission to establish a manufacturing site at Farnborough.

When work began the designers opted for a material that had proved successful in balloon construction – goldbeaters' skin. It had the advantage of being light and the disadvantage of being very expensive. In the first trial they used five layers for the envelope, but that proved too heavy to be lifted from the ground. They then tried again with just a triple layer. Things seemed to be going well but they found that they had exhausted the budget and the War Office refused to put up any more money. It must have been hugely frustrating for Templer and his team to find the army pulling the plug just when they seemed to be making real progress – and very short sighted. For a time, any developments would have to come from a different source.

The aeronaut Stanley Spencer designed a small craft, a mere 75 ft long and 20 ft diameter and the power source was equally modest – a 3½ horse power engine that drove a 10 ft. diameter wooden propeller. With such a small craft and limited power, the aviator had to squeeze into a four-foot square basket slung beneath

Willow 1 Britain's first successful airship.

the envelope. The first successful flight took place from Crystal Palace and flew over West London for over an hour and a half before landing at Eastcote, then a village on the western edge of London. As with other craft at this time it suffered from low power that made it almost impossible to make headway against even the slightest breeze. Nevertheless, Spencer continued to make other flights and was sufficiently encouraged to make a larger version that was not a great success. He continued to use it but simply as a balloon without the power.

The most successful British pioneer was Ernest T. Willows, born in Cardiff in 1888, where his father was a dentist. He was educated at Clifton College, Bristol but left at the age of fifteen with the intention of following his father's profession. He became fascinated by the idea of building an airship and he began his first project in 1904 building a ship 74 ft. long powered by a 7 horse power Peugeot engine. The following year he took off in his ship *Willows 1* from Cardiff and enjoyed an 85 minute uneventful flight. He learned a good deal from the experience and used his new knowledge in the design of *Willows 2*, larger and more powerful. He obviously had a flare for publicity for on one flight he landed his craft right outside the city hall in Cardiff. He went on making improvements and redesigned the craft, renaming it *City of Cardiff*. In 1910 he set off to fly from London to Paris – the first flight across the Channel in that direction. It did not go quite according to plan. During the night he dropped all his maps overboard and then began experiencing trouble. He made an emergency landing near Douai. With the aid of a French aviator he was able to put matters right and finished his journey to Paris on 28 December, celebrating the success by flying round the Eiffel Tower.

Willows now concentrated on his aviation business, moving to Birmingham where he built his fourth airship that had its first flight in 1912 and which was bought by the navy for £1,050 – slightly more than £100,000 today. This was quite enough for him to be able to set up another new business – a balloon school at Welsh Harp in London. He also constructed a four-seater airship to provide tourist trips over the capital. When war broke out he manufactured kites and barrage balloons. He returned to his old business after the war but died in a balloon accident in 1926. The airship he sold to the Navy was His Majesty's Naval Airship Number Two. It was shortly before that the military finally got into the idea that airships might be useful after all.

The naval authorities agreed to start constructing a rigid-framed airship and awarded the contract to the famous engineering firm Vickers, with a commitment that they would be awarded future contracts if all went well. It was to be very much a joint venture under the control of Lieutenant Usborne of the Admiralty and C.G. Robertson of Vickers. They were very influenced by German ideas and a construction shed was set up next to an existing dock at the Vickers base at Barrow-in-Furness. Officially known as Royal Naval Airship Number One, she was more generally referred to simply as *Mayfly*. Given the notoriously short life of that insect, the name was to prove all too apt. The ship would be towed out onto a floating platform for launch, much like the Zeppelin arrangement on Lake Constance. Work went steadily ahead with a number of wind tests while the craft was tethered and on 24 November 1911 the ship was ready for the first flight. It was destined never to happen. As the great craft began to emerge from the construction shed, a great gust of wind caught the front end, slamming it against the shed wall and snapping the whole in two. Unlike the persevering von Zeppelin, the Admiralty dropped the idea of airship construction and Vickers – who had a ten-year contract – also withdrew. Which is how the Willows' ship became the first in service, but not the first to be built.

It was to be 1913 before a new Admiralty department took up airship design again, and one of the leaders of the design team was a young engineer called Barnes Wallis, later to become famous for the dambuster raids of the Second World War. Just because airships were again being built did not mean that the powers that be were enthusiasts. One of the most sceptical of all was the First Lord of the Admiralty, Winston Churchill. However, in 1913 he reluctantly agreed to see a demonstration flight by naval airship number 3 called *Astra*, from a site near the mouth of the Medway. Usborne, now promoted to Lieutenant Commander, took control of the expedition with the help of a young officer recently recruited to the naval wing, T. R. Cave-Brown-Cave. The latter wrote his own account of the flight that is well worth quoting at length, as it gives a very vivid picture of the problems and dangers faced by all these early aviators.

'At dawn of the great day there was dense fog. We left Farnborough in *Astra* at about 6.30 a.m. with the intention of following the Southern Railway to London and then the river to Grain at the mouth of the Medway. The fog was so thick that we could see the railway only at intervals. We spotted a station at which the line was crossed by a large road. Was it Wimbledon or, as Usborne thought, Sutton? He turned North to find the river and immediately looking slightly upwards, we saw a tree which must have been on Wimbledon Common. Then we found the river. There was still dense fog and the next thing we saw was the water tower on Shooter's Hill. From this definite fix, Usborne set course for Chatham where the shape of the river is distinctive. By the greatest good luck we got a sight of the foundations of the new airship shed being built at Kingsnorth halfway between Chatham and Sheerness. This was quite unique. The time was 9.30 a.m. which gave us 30 mins in which to do nine miles to Grain. We saw Kingsnorth long enough to make a reliable estimate of windspeed and direction. Usborne, therefore, decided to fly very slowly and silently to a point slightly to windward of Grain, from which he would drift in complete silence. We could see nothing at 10 a.m. so Usborne made, by the bellows fog horn, the code signal asking permission to anchor. We were so close to the party waiting for us that the reply came at once by word of mouth – 'Anchor immediately'. We let go the trail rope which was 300 ft long, the end reached the ground and was found by the landing party who hauled us down.'

I trained and qualified as an air navigator many years ago and the account leaves me astonished. These men had none of the instruments available even in my day, yet somehow, they not only managed to plot an accurate course in the worst possible conditions but contrived to arrive at their rendezvous precisely on time. It impresses me and it certainly impressed Churchill. One can imagine the party at Grain peering into the fog and probably wondering whether they were wasting their time even turning up in such conditions. Then right on time, out of the mist came the blast of the foghorn. It was a demonstration of great flying skill and, even more importantly, a spectacular demonstration that the airship really was a craft with a future. Even so, there was no great rush into production and in the pre-war years the airship programme never came close to matching that of Germany.

The Army returned to airship construction when Colonel John Capper took over command of the Farnborough Balloon Factory, following the retirement of Colonel Templer. There was a new development and a new man at Farnborough – Samuel Franklin Cody. He was an American whose real name was Cowdrey but changed it when he began a career in show business as a 'sharp shooter and cowboy'. He no doubt hoped that the punters would assume he was related to the famous Buffalo Bill Cody. However, he developed a different interest apart from being a stage cowboy and thanks to a highly successful production called *The Klondyke Nugget* he began to develop a range of man-carrying flights. He devised a system whereby the kite would be tethered and could carry a man up to a height where he could act as an observer, in much the same way as the balloons had been used. He wrote to the War Office in Britain offering his services and was given a post at Farnborough. He was sufficiently astute to recognise that his kites could be transformed into powered aircraft. He acquired an Antoinette engine from France and installed it in a kite. On the nineteenth September 1907 it took off with Cody at the controls of what was now officially designated British Army Aeroplane No. 1. That same year, a few months before that initial flight, Colonel Capper managed to persuade the War Office to come up with £2,000 for airship development. He at once turned to Cody for help with various design features for the new craft based on his experience with kites.

The first airship was 122 ft. long, 26 ft. in diameter and had a capacity of 55,00 cu. ft. There was a large rudder at the rear and a smaller elevator at the bow, both based on Cody kite designs and, like Cody's aeroplane, it was powered by a 50 horse power Antoinette engine, driving two metal propellers. The gondola, suspended from netting draped over the envelope, can best be described as basic. The first tentative flight was a mere short hop of little more than half a mile. It was, however, sufficiently promising for the craft to be officially named as British Army Dirigible No.1 and given the name *Nulli Secundus*. British Army officers were almost exclusively ex public school boys, well versed in Latin – and it sounded less boastful and more classical than simply being called Second to None. Other flights were made in the area in some secrecy, but inevitably news got out that something exciting was happening at Farnborough. The press was soon snooping around but Capper kept everything very hush hush until he was ready to go public – and when he did, he did so in style.

At this stage Germany was already announcing that a Zeppelin would be making a 24-hour flight before being taken over by the army. The Kaiser was in London visiting Edward VII, so it seemed the ideal opportunity for a demonstration that anything Germany could do Britain could do just as well. It was time to wave the Union Jack and Capper announced that he and Cody would be flying an airship across central London. On the morning of Saturday 5 October 1907 they set off from Farnborough and were soon cruising along at a height of 800 feet at 16 mph being tracked by the ground crew who were following in Cody's motor car. By midday they were over Shepherd's Bush. Being a Saturday and a half day for many workers the streets were crowded. The sight of

The Navy airship, known as the *Mayfly,* broken in half by a strong wind when leaving the hangar.

the ship passing overhead was sensational and down below there was a scrum as people pushed their way through the crowds in an attempt to follow the progress of the craft. Soon they were over Hyde Park and heading for Buckingham Palace where it was hoped the king would bring out his German guests to impress them with this show of British technology, but no one appeared.

They had dropped a note to the ground crew to tell them of their plans to circle St. Paul's Cathedral, which they duly did and then set off to head back to base. Unfortunately, they hit a head wind that slowed them down to such an extent that it was clear they would never make Farnborough. Instead they decided to head south across the Thames for the open space of Clapham Common. In theory the ground crew would reach there at the same time, but the streets were so crowded with eager Londoners following their progress, they were severely delayed. As a result, the sappers were nowhere in sight. Capper threw out trail ropes and shouted to the crowd to grab them, but all they did was wave and cheer, not having the least idea what they were supposed to do. There was nothing for it but to go on and try and find an alternative landing site, and the best possibility seemed to be Crystal Palace football ground. It would have been ideal, but unfortunately they arrived in the middle of a match. It is said that twenty-one players stopped in their tracks and stared up at this apparition, while the twenty second used the opportunity to kick the ball into the net. There seems to be no record on whether or not the goal was allowed. However, the ground manager at least understood the situation and directed them to a landing in the nearby cycling stadium where they settled down without mishap. The weather failed to improve so the flight was abandoned and the airship had to be returned to Farnborough by road.

The experiment had been sufficiently successful for work to start on a second airship, named less imaginatively *Beta*. She was not a great success. At 84 ft. long and 24ft 8in. in diameter this was a tubby affair and it soon became apparent that the proportions were quite wrong for successful flight. The next problem occurred when two 8 horse power engines were installed that proved inadequate for the job. Major alterations were made. The length was increased by twenty feet and the two engines were replaced by a single 35 horse power engine. The changes worked out well and the craft was soon taking part in army manoeuvres, flying both by day and by night. When the next in line, *Gamma,* went into production it was more than twice the size of *Beta* with a capacity of 72,000 cu. ft against just 33,000 cu. ft. A more powerful 80 horse power engine was installed, driving twin propellers, mounted on swivels to assist in controlling both ascent and descent. The envelope was now of rubberised cotton, replacing the expensive goldsmiths' skin of earlier craft.

There were inevitable teething troubles with establishing a brand-new airship fleet, when everything was still very much at the experimental trial and error stage. By 1910 with work advancing on both aircraft and airships, a Parliamentary Air Defence Committee was formed and the members seem to have been unimpressed by the speed of progress at Farnborough and looked across the Channel to France, where airship development appeared to be moving at a far faster rate and they recommended buying two airships, a semi-rigid Lebaudy and a non-rigid dirigible Clément-Bayard.

Adolph Clément-Bayard designed his first airship in 1908 and although it went through successful trials with the French army at the end of that year, breaking both endurance and speed records, the army refused to buy it as they considered it too expensive. It was bought instead by the Russian army. More airships followed and were taken up by the French army and it was one of these that the British proposed to purchase. The War Office was not enthusiastic but was persuaded to accept it, though they made stiff conditions, including the ability to fly at 32 mph with a full crew on board and that when moored it should be able to withstand winds up to 20 mph. If it met those conditions, they would accept it into service. They were not, however, prepared to foot the entire bill. In the event a huge public fund-raising operation got under way led by the *Daily Mail.* £6,000 was raised towards the purchase and a further £6,000 for building a hangar to house it. The ship took off from France on 16 October 1910, crossing the Channel to land at Wormwood Scrubs and averaging a speed of 41 mph – at least satisfying one of the War Office's conditions. It was a promising beginning but once the Farnborough crew got to inspect the craft they discovered that it was in such an appalling condition that it was totally unusable. £18,000 had been spent on what turned out to be a total wreck. When one considers how hard the experts had to fight to get a paltry £2,000 for development, one might conclude that such matters were not best solved by committees. However, there was still the Lebaudy to come and perhaps, everyone hoped, there would be a better outcome.

The airship arrived at Farnborough to be greeted by the ground crew and watched by a large group of military VIPs. As it was being moved into the new hangar, the officer in charge of the operation realised to his horror that the ship appeared to be larger than the entrance and brought the operation to a halt. The delay clearly annoyed one of the watching brigadiers who ordered the men to carry on regardless and as he was by far the senior officer they had no option and obeyed. The result was inevitable. The junior officer had been right and the whole of the top of the envelope was torn away. Attempts would be made to repair and re-use it, but it was never a success. The whole operation of importing French balloons had been a costly fiasco, thanks to the arrogance of one of the top brass.

In France, the military authorities were not much more helpful than they had been in Britain, but there were commercial firms developing who were far more enterprising. One of these was the *Société Astra des Constructions Aéronautiques,* more usually simply known as Astra. They had begun by making balloons and had actually manufactured the envelope for the first Clément-Bayard airship. They received an order for an airship from Henri Deutsch

The gondola of British airship *Beta II* now preserved by the Science Museum.

de la Meurthe, the *Ville de Paris* that was completed in 1906 but had to be partly rebuilt after an accident in 1907. It proved to be a very successful ship and eventually Astra were to be manufacturing airships at four different French factories. The biggest design change came when they joined forces with the Spanish engineer Leonardo Torres Quevedo.

Torres Quevedo had become interested in the problem of how to maintain the rigidity of an airship that didn't have a rigid internal frame. He published a paper on the subject as early as 1902, but he had to wait for six more years before he could put his ideas into practice. Basically, he used a flexible internal frame made up of ropes and permeable fabric curtains that would react under pressure to keep the shape and create what became known as an autorigid airship. The system resulted in an unusual trilobed envelope; in cross section it looked like the top of a club in a pack of cards. Two experimental craft were built using this system and were successful but like others in this field they did not excite the enthusiasm of the military high ups, so he took himself off to Paris where he rapidly found a more enthusiastic response from Astra. The result was a succession of Astra Torres airships. Another French company, Société Zodiac, produced a number of small airships that were mostly sent abroad, even going to customers in South America.

America, where so many innovations were changing the course of technology in the early years of the twentieth century, seemed to have little interest in airship development. There was a rather tentative effort by the army that resulted in a small non-rigid airship being constructed in 1908 and sent to Fort Myers in Florida for testing. It had a top speed of around 20 mph and an endurance of just over two hours, scarcely making it of great military value. Nevertheless, it was sent to the Army Signals Corps School at Fort Omaha, Nebraska, where a hanger was constructed, making the site the first military air base in the U.S. There are few records of how it was used, but in any case, it was scrapped in 1912.

One wealthy American did, however, have an interest in airships. Walter Wellman designed a dirigible that he hoped to use for an ambitious flight across the North Pole. Unable to get such a craft built in the States, he moved to France, where the craft was built and moved to Spitzbergen in June 1906. The airship had a capacity of 350,000 cu. ft. and was powered by two 90 horse power engines. Although it was capable of carrying a crew of six, Wellman decided to limit the numbers to four and used the rest of the space for supplies. They set off for what would have been an epic voyage, but after only three hours in flight they were faced with fierce head winds and were forced to return to their base, There, they waited for a break in the weather but it never came. Just like Andrée when he planned his balloon flight over the Arctic, they were forced to abandon the project – and unlike Andrée they never returned for a second season and another try. Instead Wellman opted for an even more ambitious scheme; he would fly the Atlantic instead.

Wellman devised a unique system, intended to keep the airship in level flight. He had a set of floats attached to a 300-foot long steel cable. These would be lowered down to rest on the water and if the craft started to rise they would be lifted clear and their weight would drag it down again. A party of six led by Wellman set off from Atlantic City on 10 October 1910. At first things went well, but then they hit bad weather and the effect was made even worse by the action of the floats. As the wind whipped the waves ever higher, so the floats bounced with them causing the craft above to pitch violently. They endured 86 hours of this – and anyone who has ever experienced an Atlantic storm will know just what a miserable 86 hours those must have been. They were not even making any headway to the east but instead found themselves off the coast of New England. Then, during a lull in the storm, they spotted an English ship. the *Trent*, ditched the airship, clambered into their lifeboat and were rescued.

Wellman abandoned his idea for long distance flying but his engineer, Melvin Vaniman, decided to continue and was convinced that a larger airship would be needed and that it would have to have a new type of light but strong material for the envelope. The North British Rubber Company, based in Edinburgh, had developed a system for applying a thin coat of rubber to a fabric in order to make it waterproof – the best-known example of their work came when they used the process to make Wellington boots. Vaniman approached Goodyear, who already had an agreement with North British, to see if they would finance the project. If it was a success, it could well provide Goodyear with a valuable new product and help propel America into the front rank of airship constructors. The company agreed and the ship was named *Akron* after the city in Ohio where the Goodyear factory was based. It was a semi-rigid vessel that was to be equipped with three propellers, two mounted on the sides driven by modified automobile engines and a third in the stern powered by an auxiliary engine. After a short test flight in November 1911, Vaniman decided to give a public demonstration of the craft, flying from Atlantic City, before setting off for Europe. A great crowd gathered to watch the spectacle, as *Akron* rose serenely into the air and began level flight. Then, just fifteen minutes after take-off, the whole craft was enveloped in a ball of fire and crashed into the sea. There were no survivors. The disaster put a temporary end to American interest in airship development. All that was to change as the western world began to move towards war.

CHAPTER TEN

Airships at War

The first inklings of what was to come in the Great War were seen when Italy sent an expeditionary force to Libya, a country that they claimed for themselves and denied its legitimacy as part of the rapidly collapsing Ottoman Empire. The Italian government and press declared that the population would rise up in support of the Italians, that the whole war would soon be over and that the cost to the exchequer would be minimal. None of these optimistic forecasts proved to be accurate and though Tripoli was captured shortly after the Italian landing in October 1911, the rest of the country offered stubborn resistance. In March 1912, two army dirigibles, *P2* and *P3*, had arrived in Africa and carried out the first reconnaissance over the Arab and Turkish forces, dropping hand grenades onto the troops below. They served as spotter airships, directing the Italian artillery and continuing their grenade attacks on enemy concentrations of troops to some effect. The Italians achieved at least a temporary success, though it is doubtful if the airships ever played more than a minor role in winning it. But it was the first indication of a new role for flying machines, whether lighter or heavier than air; they could be used as offensive weapons, not merely as airborne platforms for observers.

The role of airships during the Great War was complex. Both the Allies and the Germans had their fleets of airships in action and the control of both was divided between the navy and the army. For the most part, the two fleets, army and navy, acted independently and, on some occasions, were even reluctant to co-operate. To simplify the story, we shall be looking at these different sections as separate entities, starting with the roles of the German army forces.

Most people, if asked about the use of airships in the First World War, the first name to come up would be 'Zeppelin' and that is not unreasonable as it was Germany that was first to make effective use of the airships. Things did not, however, start well once operations began. At the very start of the war the Imperial army commandeered three commercial airships and renumbered them; *LZ22, LZ23* and *LZ25* became *ZVII, ZVIII* and *ZIX*. As Roman numerals get complex as the numbers advance, in the following

An artist's impression of a Zeppelin attack on a British train during the First World War.

text we shall stick with the usual Arabic numbers. In any case, the Germans reverted to original Zeppelin numbers when they reached what would have been *ZXIII* – no one, it was felt, would want to fly in unlucky number thirteen. The original commercial ships had two gondolas, the foremost of which held the control room and engine room, the aft was merely an engine room and in between was a glazed walkway with wickerwork chairs for the paying passengers.

Basic alterations were made to prepare them for military service The chairs were stripped out of the passenger compartment that was now adapted for carrying bombs and a simple, rather crude bomb-aiming device. A separate small compartment was created for the radio operator. Once converted, they joined the existing fleet of army airships and further airships were soon ordered, with a lightly larger capacity. At the start of hostilities, two Zeppelins were sent to the Eastern Front to support the forces attacking Russia, and three more to the west to support the German army facing the British, French and Belgian forces. They were soon to see active service.

The difficulties of using slow, low flying craft for attacks on enemy positions soon became all too apparent. In August 1914 Z6 was despatched to the Belgian fortress of Liége where three 50 kg. bombs were dropped from a low level, which at once made the ship vulnerable to fire from the ground forces. It was a target so large that it could hardly be missed as it made its ponderous retreat from the scene. The damage from small arms fire was so great that the captain had to make a forced landing in a forest clearing.

Z7 was the next casualty. German and French forces were battling over the disputed territory of Alsace, but the German command had lost contact with the French troops, so they sent the airship out to locate them and to report back on their position and movements. It was a difficult and dangerous operation as the ship set off at night, flying in a mountainous region, with peaks rising in places to over 4000 feet, uncomfortably close to the Zeppelin's cruising height. In the morning the crew spotted a detachment of French troops and dropped their bombs. They flew on and then came across a much larger concentration of forces and to assess their numbers the captain brought his ship down to under 3,000 ft. At once she attracted a barrage of artillery and rifle fire and the captain was forced to try to turn for home, but in doing so presented an even greater target. There was severe damage, but somehow the damaged ship limped on, gradually losing altitude as gas escaped through the gaping holes left from the bombardment. Long before the ship was able to make it back to base, Z7 made a forced landing in Lorraine and was wrecked.

Z8 got off to an even worse start. She had scarcely begun her flight before she came under attack, not from the French but from her own troops. Having survived that, the ship carried on and soon the crew found themselves over a considerable enemy force.

They hastily dropped all the bombs and tried to turn for home but once again the ground fire caused irreparable damage, this time so severe that the ship did not even make it back to German held territory. They crashed but the crew escaped and managed to flee before the French arrived. The last glimpse they had of their ship was of French officers slashing it to pieces with their sabres, which was perhaps not quite the most sensible thing to do to a vessel that might still have been useful if repaired.

Things on the Russian front were not going any better. Z5 was hit by a shell that damaged her rudder so that she was completely out of control. The crew managed to release their bombs, killing 23 soldiers, but then came down in a wood. The captain had died from a gunshot wound and the remainder of the crew were taken captive. It was becoming clear that slow, low flying airships were too easy a target to hit when deployed against heavily armed forces. It was time for the army to reconsider how best to deploy their rapidly diminishing resources.

The decision was taken to attack strategic targets, but it was hoped ones that would not put up such stout resistance. At this time, nowhere had prepared for aerial bombardments and consequently no anti-aircraft guns were in position. The first of these raids saw Z6 leave Köln for an attack on Antwerp. It was a success in that the craft reached the city, dropped its bombs and returned safely. Encouraged by this trial run, a whole series of raids were mounted on towns and cities in France and Belgium. The raids continued through the winter of 1914-15 and must have been miserable for the crews in the unheated gondolas. The bomb loads had been doubled, which slowed the craft down and made the journeys last even longer.

The main targets in the first months were the strategically important ports of Antwerp and Ostend that between them received almost 10,000 lbs. of bombs. By the end of 1914, however, a new type of Zeppelin was constructed, the 'n' type, with an increased capacity of 883,000 cu. ft. and three more powerful 180 horse power engines. The new craft could both fly higher than their predecessors, but also considerably faster, with a top speed of around 50 mph. With the new craft available, the German High Command decided on a new tactic. It was the head of Naval Aviation who first put forward a plan for bombing raids on England and presented it to the Kaiser. He somewhat reluctantly agreed but specified that there should be no attacks on

The British government used the Zeppelin raids on Britain in their recruitment adverts.

London itself. The city was, after all, home to many of his close relations, the British royal family. There were, however, many strategic targets on the east coast that were well within range, including important harbours and ship building centres. The task was initially entrusted to the naval airships.

The first attempt on 13 January 1915 was undertaken by four airships but bad weather forced them back before they had even reached the English coast. Six days later, a second attempt was made with three craft, one of which, *L6*, was commanded by the head of the naval aviation division, Peter Strasser. The latter was forced to turn back with engine trouble and the remaining two Zeppelins headed for the Humber and the port of Hull, each armed with ten explosive and ten incendiary bombs. The northerly wind, however, took them off track and they finished up crossing the coast in Norfolk. *L3* dropped its bombs on Great Yarmouth, killing two people and *L4* bombed King's Lynn, killing a woman and child. It was hardly a strategic triumph, but it was a foretaste of things to come, with extensive raids on the east coast – raids which inevitably brought a certain amount of fear to the civilian population. My mother was a little girl at the time, living in Stockton-on-Tees, which was then quite an important shipbuilding centre. She had clear memories of seeing a Zeppelin pass overhead and how menacingly huge it seemed.

On 12 February, the Kaiser issued a directive that now encouraged raids not just on eastern England but allowed for them over East London and the docks, but on no account were they to bomb royal places of residential areas – presumably the residents of East London didn't count.

There were a number of attempted raids on London by naval airships and then the army decided to have an attempt. The first proposed raid was to be undertaken by *Z12* under the command of Captain Ernst Lehmann. Navigation in these early days was always a tricky problem. In daytime in good visibility, life was simple; you used your maps and charts to fix your position using recognisable landmarks. At night, this was obviously more difficult and although it was possible to plot a course and then set a compass bearing, there was still the wind to take into account. A side wind would have a considerable effect on the elongated cylinder of the Zeppelin, and although the compass might show that you were pointing in one direction, thanks to the drift caused by the wind you could be travelling over the ground in a direction that was taking you well away from your intended target. There was an alternative available that had been used by navigators at sea for many years, astro-navigation based on the heavenly bodies. This worked well when taking sextant measurements from the open deck of a ship, but there was a problem when you were in a gondola slung below the huge bulk of an airship's envelope: you simply couldn't see the sky above you. These difficulties were compounded when Lehmann set off on his night flight to London on 17 March 1915 by encountering dense fog.

He set a course for England that would, he hoped, give him a fix by reaching a lighthouse on the coast. When that failed to materialise, he cruised up and down the south coast in the hope of being able to locate the Thames estuary. The occasional glimpses of land beneath him were no help in fixing his position, no sighting of the Thames was made and he had no alternative; he headed back across the Channel. He had, however, no intention of returning without achieving something. Approaching the French coast a crew member was lowered in a basket in the hope of identifying a suitable landmark. They found themselves over Calais, and it was here that they dropped their bombs. Lehmann then had the tricky task of navigating his way back to base, with little more than his compass and altimeter as guides. He eventually made a landing, still in fog, but narrowly missed the airfield, finally coming to rest on a nearby railway line, but fortunately without doing too much damage or meeting a train. In the circumstances, it could all have been much worse.

Z12 made two more attempts to bomb London but again without success. The second flight was hampered by heavy rain and again Lehmann found an alternative, this time Dunkirk. Unlike on the Calais raid, he was confronted with concentrated fire from the ground that resulted in one propeller being shot off. However, he again made it back. The third never reached its target, finishing up on the East coast of England and Lehmann dropped his bombs on Harwich. It was the first army Zeppelin raid on an English town, but certainly not the last. However, the repeated failure to hit the capital led to a change of plan: the new target would be Paris.

This time three airships were involved and their navigators were helped to keep on course by a series of coded signals flashed by searchlights under their flight path. They had to cross the battle lines of the Western Front and although they were able to fly at the height of 8,000 ft, the Schütte-Lunz ship was hit and suffered considerable damage. She turned back for home, leaving two Zeppelins to continue to Paris. This time they did reach the city and were able to cruise round looking for suitable targets, eventually settling on an electric city generating station and a factory. Both ships came under intense attack from the ground on their return.

Z10 was hit and several of the internal gas bags were punctured, but enough was left to make it back. *LZ35* was caught and followed by searchlights on the ground but managed to avoid damage. On the whole the German authorities regarded the raid as a great success.

The navy continued to carry out raids on the English coast with mixed success. Navigation was always something of a problem. The commander of the *L9* was convinced that he had inflicted considerable damage on docks round the mouth of the Tyne. Actually the river was the Wansbeck and the bombs fell round mining villages, causing virtually no important damage though two men were injured, A raid on Lowestoft was a success, setting fire to a timber yard, The other Zeppelin commander on that raid had little idea where he was but dropped his bombs on the only town he saw, which turned out to be Malden. There was a near disaster on one raid, when the *L5* ran into a hail storm. Ice formed on the envelope, forcing the craft down. The captain jettisoned his bombs and managed to gain enough height to stagger back to safety. At about this time the older Zeppelins were being retired in favour of the new, more efficient versions now being produced. With these craft it was hoped to resume the attempts to bomb London. In the event, the army got there first. Their new airships raided a

A British airship on submarine control, accompanying a warship disguised as a merchantman.

number of sites in the southeast of England, then on the night of 31 May 1915 *LZ38* finally reached the capital and dropped 3,000 lbs. of bombs. In spite of the Kaiser's injunctions to concentrate on the dock areas, they hit north east London, causing considerable damage and killing seven civilians.

The effect of the bombing raids on the actual conduct of the war was negligible but they had a huge effect on British opinion. The government mounted a propaganda campaign, emphasising the horrors of these aerial attacks on civilians to encourage recruitment into the army. By 1916, however, the defences against the attacks were steadily improving. There were more anti-aircraft guns in position and fighter plane development had been very rapid. Two vital factors were the introduction of the synchronised machine gun that could be fired forward through the gaps as the propeller turned and the incendiary bullet. The gun made accurate aiming far simpler – basically the pilot pointed his plane at the target. Previously, although aircraft had shot at the Zeppelins, they seldom managed to do more harm than to puncture one or two of the gas bags, but still leaving enough hydrogen to keep the craft aloft. The effect of the new bullets would be devastating.

On Monday 4 September 1916, three aircraft of the Royal Flying Corps set off in pursuit of airship *SL11*. The airship attempted to get away by diving then ascending to a height of around 12,000 feet, while firing its own machine guns at the RFC planes. One of the pilots, Lieutenant William Robinson, anticipated the manoeuvre and managed to close in on the ship and rake it with gunfire. The incendiary bullets hit home and in seconds the hydrogen had exploded. Robinson was awarded the Victoria Cross, the citation reading: 'For most conspicuous bravery. He attacked an enemy airship under conditions of great difficulty and danger, and sent it crashing to the ground a flaming wreck. He had been in the air for more than two hours and had previously attacked another airship during his flight.' The loss of the *SL11* was enough to persuade the army to abandon its attacks on Britain, However, the navy continued its attacks right up to August 1918. The raids over Britain resulted in considerable damage but were not the crippling blow that had been hoped for, but they did have one important side effect; a large number of RFC fighter aircraft were tied to the home front instead of being available for use in continental Europe.

It was easy for the British people to assume that they were the main targets for all Zeppelin raids, but in fact they represented only a portion of the sorties made during the war years. The army had originally deployed its airships on the Western Front but the heavy losses brought that to an end. They had far more success, however, on the Eastern Front. Initially just three airships were sent east. *SLII* was sent to the support of the Austro-Hungarian army, while the two Zeppelins were very active further north. *Z4* hit a number of important targets, such as railway junctions and marshalling yards causing considerable disruption to the Russian troop transport system. On one raid it was so badly damaged by ground fire that it had to be withdrawn and returned to Germany for use in training crew. *Z5* was less fortunate. After flying several successful reconnaissance missions, she was brought down by artillery fire and the crew captured. Replacements were brought in and the raids on transport systems were continued, until the losses began to mount just as they had on the Western Front. At this point the army decided to abandon their whole airship fleet, handed the surviving craft to the navy and concentrated on developing heavier than air craft.

The navy airships were a vital component in the war at sea. Their primary role was as reconnaissance craft, but they were armed with both machine guns and bombs and were quite ready to take on a combat role if circumstances demanded it. This was demonstrated very effectively on 15 December 1914, when *L5* and *L6* set off to search for British ship movements near Heligoland. Instead they found British aircraft mounting a raid on Nordholz. At this stage of the war, the airships had better arms than the fighters, but the more easily manoeuvred and faster aircraft were easily able to avoid any direct conflict. The captain of *L5* realised that to have reached this far into the North Sea they must have been based on an aircraft carrier, so set off to follow their track. He came across the carrier and found two of the seaplanes still on the water, waiting to be picked up. He attacked with bombs and machine gun fire and completely destroyed them. Meanwhile *L6* came across British mine layers. Unfortunately, the radio was not working so they were unable to pass on the information to the German fleet. Two escorting cruisers now appeared on the scene and the Zeppelin went on the attack. Bombs were dropped but failed to hit their target and the airship turned for home and arrived safely back at base. In its essentials this had been a very successful trip, demonstrating the value of reconnaissance flights and showing the attack capabilities of airships. The result could have been an even greater success but for the equipment failure. These were early days, radios were still primitive and bomb aiming was, to put it mildly, an inexact science.

The reconnaissance work was by far the most important and the most successful part of German airship operations in the war. Before the war began, both sides had built up substantial fleets and everyone expected a series of major engagements at sea. In the event, there was to be just the one major engagement, the Battle of Jutland in 1916 that led to terrible losses on both sides. The British lost 14 battleships and the Germans 14, but far more horrific was the loss of life: 6,784 British sailors and 3,039 Germans. After the indecisive battle the German Imperial Fleet was largely confined to port, enabling Britain to maintain a naval blockade in the North Sea. That did not mean there was nothing for the airships to do. Aircraft carriers were used to a large extent by the British to mount attacks on the German mainland and, as on the flight of *L5* if they were spotted in time, the raid could be thwarted, either by direct action, catching aircraft before take-off or by calling up more powerful forces. Statistics give a good idea of the relative importance of bombing missions and reconnaissance flights. Altogether the navy had 78 airships that notched up almost 20,000 hours of flying time and covered just over 800,000 miles. Of the 1554 sorties flown, 1148 were reconnaissance flights. The losses, however, were high; 52 were lost, 26 to enemy action and a total of 436 men lost their lives. This was not a large number compared to the carnage in the trenches, but it was a substantial proportion of the aircrew.

In Britain, military airships were all but unknown following the fiasco of the attempted launch of *Mayfly*. Arguments for building a rigid airship were ignored by the authorities on the grounds that no one knew how to fly them – a strange argument as very few people knew how to fly aeroplanes either. Early attempts were made to buy in airships from Germany and Italy but the approach of war prevented them being delivered. In June 1914 the decision was taken that airships would all be under the command of a new Royal Naval Air Service, and the few that were held by the army were handed over. The latter was to concentrate on aeroplanes, eventually leading to the formation of the Royal Flying Corps (RFC). At the start of the war there was a grand total of two rigid airships, an Astra-Torres and a German Parseval that were at once placed on duty patrolling the coast. There were five non-rigids, now usually referred to as 'blimps'. It soon, however, became apparent that there was an urgent need for airships to face a new menace, the German submarines, the U-boats. The British naval blockade was effectively stopping supplies reaching Germany from other countries; now the Germans were equally keen to cut off supplies to Britain. The threat to British shipping was obvious and the country depended on imports for all kinds of vital commodities, not least food. In the early twentieth century, the country imported 75 per cent of its wheat, 50 per cent of its meat and 25 per cent of its butter. Spotting submarines from on board a ship was next to impossible as the submarines could simply disappear below the surface if warships were in the area. They could, however, be spotted from above and the only craft with the endurance to go out on long submarine searches was the airship.

Faced with this threat, the Admiralty ordered an immediate construction programme and to save both time and money they were to be as cheap and simple as possible. They were small blimps designated as 'Submarine Scouts' and given SS prefixes. The first generation were just 143 foot long with a capacity of 60,000 cu. ft. Instead of making special gondolas, the fuselage of a B.E.2c was slung underneath. The plane itself was a development of a biplane that had first entered service in 1912 powered by a tractor engine. The blimp may have been very basic but it was effective with a top speed of around 50 mph and able to stay aloft for up to sixteen hours. Altitude was not a problem, as it needed to fly comparatively low for its spotting duties. The crew consisted of the pilot and a wireless operator to relay any sightings to the fleet. They also carried bombs that could be deployed if they were lucky enough to catch a submarine on the surface. Altogether twenty-nine of these craft were constructed.

The U-boats were at their most vulnerable when they had to make their way through the English Channel. Submerged they were all but invisible, but all submarines had to surface at intervals to recharge their batteries and in order to spot their targets they had to come close to the surface to raise the periscopes above the waves. On the surface, they were, of course, easy to spot. On one occasion, in December 1917, *SSZ* was on patrol and spotted a submarine in the distance but was uncertain whether it was friend or foe. The airship sent out a radio message for a naval vessel to come to the scene and soon received an unmistakable identification from the submarine as the crew began shooting at them. The airship went on the attack, dropping bombs as the U-boat dived. A flare was dropped over the site so that the navy could finish the job.

When looking out for merchant ships to attack, the submarine periscope left its own signature on the surface of the sea, a long feather-like wake. It was almost invisible from surface craft but was easily seen from an airship that could at once report its position. The SS ships were out on regular patrols looking for any of these signs. Later in the war, the Admiralty finally realised that convoys offered better protection than ships travelling on their own. There was some doubt as to the value of the airships, some naval officers arguing that because an airship could be easily seen it pinpointed the convoy's position. The airships' supporters pointed out that it also acted as a deterrent and, even if an attack was made, the airship was perfectly placed to bring vessels and their lethal depth charges to exact retribution.

Submarines were not the only threat to the merchantmen. Mines were equally lethal. They were difficult to spot from a ship, often only spotted when it was too late to change course. They could, however, be seen from the air. Squadron Leader T.P. York-Moore was an airship pilot in the latter years of the war and wrote an account of his experiences that was quoted in Lord Ventry and Eugene M. Koleśnik's *Airship Saga*, 1982. He served for a time in the Dardanelles campaign. On 15 October 1916 he was out on patrol:

> 'I spotted a line of nine mines from a height of 300 ft. the surface of the sea was rippled, and I could see every detail of each mine – chains, nuts, horns and so on. Three days later a signal was received from SNO Salonica: "Thanks to the report from the Kassandra airship, nine mines have been destroyed off Panomi Point which is very creditable to the airship's crew concerned, whose names are to be forwarded to SNO Salonica".'

Later he was posted to the very busy airship field at Mullion in Cornwall. It was on a flight from there while shepherding a convoy of American troop ships that he saw a mine directly ahead of the leading ship. 'I semaphored and megaphoned to her CO, but she did not alter course until I fired a burst at the mine with my Lewis gun. She then took evasive action.' Similar stories could be told by many airship pilots and many lives must have been saved.

The SS series of airships had their limitations, though they were developed over the years. By the end of 1915 fifty of the class had been completed and a larger airship now went into production. They were designated as C for Coastal and had a capacity of 160,000 cu. ft.

Powered by two 180 horse power Sunbeam engines they could stay on patrol for over twenty four hours. They carried a crew of five, one of whom occupied a lonely position on top of the envelope, manning a machine gun. A later version, the C* class, was even bigger and had a top speed of around 60 mph The final stage of development came with the NS – North Sea – Class, with a capacity of 360,000 cu. ft. They were powered by a pair of 240 horse power engines and had even greater endurance. One of these craft, the *NS11*, created a record for non-rigid airships by staying up for over 61 hours. This endurance gave the airships great scope in their hunts for mines and submarines. The craft had an enclosed gondola, able to carry a crew of ten, which allowed them to work in shifts of five men, each working for twelve hours. They also found a most unusual role in protecting against enemy air attacks. A special rig was constructed beneath the envelope to which a Sopwith Camel biplane could be attached. It could carry the plane quickly up to altitude and release it the moment it was needed for combat. It did have limitations, however, for it could not take the plane far from its base. Once released there was no mechanism for picking it up again, so the plane had to be able to make its way back to the airfield.

Throughout the war, the British relied almost entirely on their blimps, but in 1916 the Admiralty decided to commission a rigid airship. Vickers, who had begun the whole process before the war, had produced a design named the *R9* but it had never gone into production. Now Short Brothers were invited to build ships based on this pattern. Ideas had changed in the intervening years and a number of modifications were needed before they were ready to go ahead with *R31* and *R32*, both of which were constructed using a wooden rather than metal frame. The rigid airship could be made far bigger than any blimp and *R31* was massive by comparison with even the NS class; 615 feet long with a capacity of 1,547,000 cu. ft. and powered by six 275 horse power Rolls Royce engines, later reduced to five. She had a speed of 70 mph. The vessel was heavily armed with machine gun positions on top of the hull, in the stern, in the gondola and in the walkway that stretched from the gondola to the stern. This was an imposing fighting machine and early trials were successful but as she set out for delivery, everything went wrong. She took off from the airfield at Cardington in Bedfordshire where a special, large hangar had been constructed – and still survives. In flight, the internal wooden frame that was glued together began to come apart and after a hasty landing on a wet day, the whole structure collapsed.

Vickers also built five rigid airships in the last year of the war, rather slower and smaller than the Short Brothers version. One of them did actually become involved in an action against a submarine, helping to sink a German U-boat in the very last week of the year. But the rigid airships played a small part in the conflict, compared with the fleet of almost 400 blimps that flew right through the war.

The French had been among the leading airship designers in the pre-war years and when hostilities began they had a fleet of fifteen. The *Fleurus* was the first into action on 9 August 1914 and carried out a successful raid. Other airships were considerably less fortunate. The *Conté* set off the same day but came under intense fire from the ground and limped back to base with over a thousand bullet holes – not as a result of enemy action but all inflicted by France's own troops. The *Depuy-de-Lôme* did manage a bombing raid, but on 24 August the enthusiastic French troops once again let loose, this time not only damaging the craft but tragically killing one of the crew. Next it was the turn of the *Montgolfier* to be fired on by their own side and it was forced down, happily on this occasion with no loss of life. The airship crews must have felt a lot safer attacking the enemy than they were flying over their friends. Ships were repaired and went back into service, but still suffered far more from French gunfire than from German. The slow, low flying airships were certainly tempting targets and given the damage that

A United States Navy B-class non-rigid airship. Officially designated B-limps, they became simply Blimps.

was being inflicted, all flights were halted in January 1915 and only resumed in April when more advanced airships became available.

When operations resumed, a signalling system was put in place that was intended to stop French troops firing at their own craft. It was only partially successful – they still managed to down the *Coutelle* on only its third operational mission that September. Other craft were luckier in escaping the French sharp shooters and bigger and better were coming into service. The Astra-Torres *Alsace* made a number of successful night raids but on one of these the moon shone brightly, making her an easy target for the German gunners. She was forced down and one crew member was killed and the other six captured. It was clear that on the battlefield of Europe, it was the gunners on the ground who now had the upper hand. The only defence was to have ships that were bigger, could fly higher and faster. However, like the British, the French now took the sensible course of concentrating their resources in the navy, where the airships were far more effective. It was agreed that the army ships would all be turned over to the Navy, but when the transfer day arrived the Army losses had been so high that only the *D'Arlandes* was left in an airworthy condition. And it was not only the airships that had suffered damage, far too many experienced crew had lost their lives as well. The French built more airships and also bought SS types from Britain. Part of the fleet was now based in the English Channel and part in the Mediterranean and North Africa, where they played a valuable role as convoy escorts.

The only other country to have an active fleet throughout the war was Italy. At the start they had eight non-rigid ships built by the engineering corps and three semi-rigids built by Forlarninis. There was a small contribution made towards helping with anti-submarine patrols, but the main effort was put into daytime reconnaissance flights over the Austrian lines. This made them vulnerable to attacks both from the ground and from German fighter planes and a terrible toll was taken. In 1917 three craft were shot down, with the loss of two crew members and two more were destroyed when a hangar was bombed. Somehow or other, the remaining crews managed to carry on, flying their dangerous missions across enemy lines right up to the end of the war.

No other country made significant use of airships throughout the war, but the United States did so when they finally became involved in the conflict in April 1917. Their airship programme had got off to a rather tentative start in 1916 when the US Navy built a small blimp based on the successful British SS types. It was intended as a one off to be used in experimenting how such craft could best be used, but when in 1917 it became clear that war was more than likely to be declared an order went out to start at once on constructing sixteen non-rigid airships. The envelopes were to be built by Goodyear and the training site for the completed craft was at Wingfoot Lake close to the factory at Akron. The Curtiss Aeroplane and Motor Corporation built the gondolas. The craft were 163 ft. long with a capacity of 84,00 cu. ft. and a maximum speed of 47 mph They did, however, have a considerable range of almost a thousand miles.

The engineers in charge of the first blimp B1, Ralph Upson and Lt. Preston, also took charge of her for the maiden flight. Because the facilities at Wingfoot Lake were not yet ready, the initial flight took place on 24 May 1917 from the White City Amusement Park in Chicago. The first flight went well and more tests were flown. On the fourth, which set off at midnight on 29 May, Upson decided not to return to the Amusement Park but set off instead for Wingfoot Lake, but had to make a forced landing at Medina due to a problem with the oil. In spite of the interruption it still took the record for the longest flight yet made in the country.

Work went ahead on the remaining B-Class airships that went into service patrolling the East Coast. By this time the U-boats were looking to attack shipping closer to the American mainland. One of the B-Class, flying out from Chatham, Mass., did locate an enemy submarine and called up seaplanes for an attack. On a separate occasion two of the craft located a U-boat about to start laying mines in the entrance to New York harbour and drove it off. Although none of the US navy airships was ever sent to Europe, crews did go over and were permitted to use French craft on patrol duties. The US navy may have played a minor role in Europe but the B-Class did a splendid job in protecting shipping off the American coast, clocking up 13,500 hours of flying time.

By the time the war ended, airships had more than proved their value but it was equally clear that they had limitations. The advances in aircraft design over the four years had been far greater than any made in developing airships and most military authorities were happy to declare the airship as obsolete. They could never match the new aircraft for either speed or manoeuvrability and that made them all too vulnerable. They did, however, have one huge advantage over their heavier than air competitors: they had a far greater range. And that was the factor that would give them a future in the world of civilian aviation.

CHAPTER ELEVEN

Airships in Peacetime

Count Von Zeppelin had died in 1917 and the business was taken over by his nephew, Barn Gemmingen, working with Hugo Eckener. At the end of the war, the company was manufacturing what would have been *L72*. They were very fortunate to have even the vestiges of a company to run. The intention was that all military German airships should be handed over to the victorious European powers, but many Germans saw this as a betrayal and an insult. When the German battleships anchored in Scapa Flow off Orkney were scuttled to prevent them being used by the British, a group decided on a similar action to wreck airships. The craft had mostly been deflated and hung up in sheds at Nordholz and Wittmundhaven. The conspirators released them so that they fell to the ground and were irreparably damaged. The Allies at once demanded that all remaining airships be handed over and that the factory at Friedrichshafen be permanently closed. At this point the Americans stepped in and pointed out that they were ordering an L-type airship for their navy and would object very strongly to the closure which would prevent it being built. The American case was strengthened by the fact that none of the confiscated airships had been allotted to them. The factory remained open and Zeppelin continued to manufacture airships.

Zeppelin were left with a factory and a single craft under construction, the one that would have been sent to the Navy as *L72* but now it was hoped that they could keep it and convert it to civilian use as *LZ114*. There was also an ambitious plan to kick start the new venture by an audacious attempt to be the first to fly the Atlantic, using *LZ114*. They received permission from the German government to go ahead with the plan but decided not to incur problems in advance by not applying for any further permissions from other countries. The plans were hatched in considerable secrecy – even the flight was to be a bit cloak and dagger. The intention was to fly out into the English Channel at night, then turn to head for America, and only then, when they were well under way, would they ask permission to land in the United States. Inevitably such a complex scheme could never really be kept under wraps. News leaked out and an order appeared from the German government, cancelling their permission to make the flight. No reason was given, but the likeliest explanation was that the victorious powers had no intention of allowing such a high prestige flight to be undertaken by their recently defeated enemy. Zeppelin were not, after all, to have the honour of being the first to fly the Atlantic as we shall see later.

Zeppelin plans received a further setback when *LZ114* was also commandeered and handed over to the French. It must have been very galling for the German engineering team to see that their craft, now renamed *Dixmude* after a city in Belgium, was to go on to make a record-breaking flight over the Mediterranean. The ship stayed aloft for 118 hours, covering approximately 8,000 kilometres. It was all too clear that, had they been allowed to try, the German crew could indeed have reached the United States.

Zeppelin were now starting again from scratch, though it was not altogether bad news. They no longer had to try and adapt military aircraft but could begin on new designs specifically aimed at long distance passenger services. Development began on a new 'y' Class intended specifically for a service that had been agreed with

R34 at the Mineola airfield near New York, after completing her flight across the Atlantic.

a Swedish company for flights to link Berlin and Stockholm, the two operating alternately. The new airships were not as big as their military predecessors, but with four 245 horse power engines they had an impressive top speed of over 80 mph and a range of over a thousand miles. They were designed for a crew of sixteen and a maximum of twenty-one passengers. Before the Swedish flights got under way, the first of the new airships, the *Bodensee*, began to operate between Friedrichshafen and Berlin. The flight time was six hours compared with eighteen by train and there was no shortage of customers. Indeed, the first 103 flights carried 2,450 passengers, an average of 23.8 per flight – above the intended load. Everything seemed to be going well and the second craft was completed when there was another dramatic change in fortunes.

The Treaty of Versailles, signed in June 1919, levied punitive reparation payments on Germany. The victorious Allies were more intent on making Germany pay for the horrors of the war than they were on ensuring the country would be able to recover and take a positive role in a Europe that would once again be at peace. The effects on the German economy were disastrous and Zeppelin were among the first companies to be affected. *Bodensee* and its successor *LZ121* were both confiscated, the former being sent to Italy, the latter to France. Once again, the company had to make a fresh start and it says a good deal for their perseverance that they didn't simply throw in the towel and abandon the whole business. They could only watch as other companies took over the process they had begun. As an added irritation, the first transatlantic flight was made by a British airship, the design of which was based on an original by Zeppelin.

In 1916, the Zeppelin *L33* had set out on a bombing raid over England but had crashed in East Anglia. There was not much damage done, so for the first time British engineers had a chance to study the very latest design ideas that were being put into practice in Germany. They made use of the information to create two craft, *R33* and *R34*. These were impressive craft, with a length of 643 ft. and a diameter of 79 ft., powered by five 275 horse power engines. *R34* was based at the RAF station at East Fortune, near Edinburgh, a base for the newly formed Royal Air Force Airship Section. Early in the morning of 2 July 1919 she set off, with Major G. H. Scott in charge of a crew of thirty to fly to New York. It was only after they were under way that a stowaway was discovered. An aircraftman called Ballantyne had been desperate to make the flight as one of the crew and, when he wasn't selected, decided to go anyway.

Once over the Atlantic, the crew met rain clouds but they were easily able to rise above them and continue a comfortable flight until just after midday on 4 July, they crossed the Canadian coast in Nova Scotia and turned south for New York. After that their luck turned as they ran into a serious storm that they were quite unable to avoid, unable to get above the towering thunder clouds. Being in an electric storm when the only thing that is keeping you from disaster is a large quantity of inflammable gas can hardly have been an enjoyable experience. Major Scott was sufficiently concerned as to make arrangements for an emergency landing in Massachusetts but the situation improved, the wind blew in their favour and they arrived over New York early on the afternoon of 6 July. To make sure there were no last-minute problems as the craft prepared to land, one of the crew, Major J.E.M. Pritchard, parachuted down to Minneola airfield to supervise the landing arrangements. There was a large crowd waiting and a grandstand had been erected for all those who had come to witness the end of this historic flight.

The arrival of an airship in New York caused a huge amount of interest and the crew were detained for three days celebrating their success and giving a seemingly endless procession of interviews. Then, at 3.54 on the morning of 10 July, they set off to return home. Things didn't go entirely to plan. One of the engines broke down and there was nothing the crew could do to restart it but the airship seemed to function perfectly well without it. Crossing the Irish coast, they received weather reports that indicated that their best plan rather than head for London as originally planned was to return to East Fortune. However, before they arrived they received another message directing them to Pulham in Norfolk, where they arrived safely on the 13th. It had been a remarkable round trip and would have received huge publicity if they had been the first to fly the Atlantic. They were not; Alcock and Brown had beaten them to it, flying from St. John's Newfoundland in a Vickers Vimy IV bomber and landing in Ireland on 15 June. But the RAF team had the satisfaction of being the first to make a crossing from east to west and the first to make a round trip. More importantly they had demonstrated that an airship was perfectly capable of operating on what was potentially the most lucrative passenger route in the world, between Europe and America.

Scott was responsible for one of the most important innovations of those years, the mooring mast. The device was described by

Major General Hjalmar Riiser-Larsen, who was training to become an airship pilot and his succinct description could scarcely be bettered.

> 'A wire from a winch on the ground is carried up on the inside of the mast and out on to a swivel arm at the top of the mast. This swivel arm ends in a hollow cup that fits a corresponding cone in the bow of the airship. The wire is taken through this down to the ground and pulled about 325 ft. to the leeward of the mast. A shackle is then fixed to the end of the wire. Instead of an ordinary cordage bow rope, the airship has a wire one. When the airship is conveniently placed, this mooring cable is lowered, the ground crew couple the wires together a signal to the captain when the coupling has been made. The captain then discharges a little water ballast from the bow to hold it up when the weight of the wire becomes evident. Heaving in from the ground follows and the springs are released, the ship's cone is hauled down into the hollow 'cup' on the receiving arm and the airship is then fast.'

This triumphant Atlantic flight did not mark a new beginning for airships in the Royal Air Force but rather it was to be the last great exploit. The Airship Service continued in existence, but with the war at an end there was little enthusiasm for building new craft. The orders for *R35* were cancelled, but the *R36* was already being built by Beardsmore and the *R37* by Short Brothers. The *R37* was not completed when the Airship Service was disbanded and work simply ceased. Eventually the ship was dismantled. *R36*, however, was not only finished but had already begun flight trials. It was decided to continue with a view to finding a civilian use, possibly as a spotter for the police, reporting on traffic conditions or crowd control. Things did not go well. On her delivery flight to Pulham in May 1921, two of her fins broke but the ship managed to arrive safely, in spite of suddenly and alarmingly dropping a thousand feet when the accident occurred. In August of that year she overshot the mooring mast at Pulham and suffered severe damage. There was now a major problem. The ship was not able to leave Pulham and all the available hangars were already occupied. But the weather was deteriorating and there was no question of keeping her out in the open. There was one craft that could be sacrificed, the captured Zeppelin *L64* and it was broken up and dragged away to make space for the British

craft. In the event, they need not have scarificied the Zeppelin as *R36* was destined never to fly again.

There was one other craft constructed at this time at the end of the war, the *R38*. Ordered by the Admiralty, the specifications were exact and demanding. She was required to patrol the North Sea for six days without support and be able to travel as far as 300 miles from her home base. Her armaments were impressive: she was to carry four 520 lb. bombs and eight 230 lb. bombs, together with a 1 pounder gun on top of the ship and 12 pairs of machine guns. To meet these requirements an immense airship was called for. She was 695 ft. long 85½ ft. diameter with a capacity of 2,724,00 cu. ft. Her six 350 horse power engines gave her a speed of 71 mph. She was then the largest airship in the world. Unfortunately, by the time she was completed the Admiralty no longer either needed or wanted her. However, there was a customer. The Americans not having been given a share of the confiscated Zeppelins, needed to obtain a large rigid airship from somewhere. They agreed to buy *R38* and she would then become *ZRII*.

She was launched from Cardington on 23 June 1921 and flew to Howden in Yorkshire for test flights. By the time of the fourth flight, she had already had her livery changed to her new American

The American airship *Shenandoah.*

designation and was almost ready to be flown across the Atlantic to New Jersey. That day, 23 August, she was to fly to Pulham to be prepared for the long delivery flight. On arrival in Norfolk the airfield was shrouded in fog, so it was agreed that the ship would spend the night cruising above the North Sea and try again for a landing the next morning. On her return the crew found the fog had still not lifted so they continued with their test flight. They were over the Humber near Hull, when the crew tried to make a very sharp turn. Eyewitnesses on the ground described what happened next. The air ship seemed to crumple up and then broke in two. The front section broke off and exploded, killing 44 crew members. The tail section collapsed into the sea without catching fire and five men were rescued from the wreckage. There was never a completely satisfactory explanation for the accident, but many experts now believe it can be traced back to the requirements of the wartime Zeppelins. As the attacks on the airships became more successful, the Germans felt that the best way of avoiding damage was to fly higher than ever before, and to do that they had to lose some weight from the craft. As a result, the internal metal structure was rather less robust than it had been before, but it was felt that this was still acceptable as long as the craft were not put under too many stresses. The British designers seem to have been unaware of this and as a result, when the *R38* was put through a series of manoeuvres involving sharp turns, the strain proved too great.

The effect on airship development was immediate. Short Brothers had been planning an even larger craft with a capacity of 4,450,000 cu. ft. that was intended for commercial use, capable of carrying fifty passengers and with a theoretical range of around 6,000 miles. The wreck of *R38* brought the scheme to an abrupt close. It was to be three years before anyone began to seriously consider restarting airship construction for passengers. The Americans, however, had not yet abandoned their plans for constructing rigid airships. The navy had lost fifteen of their men in the *R38* and that and other disasters may well have influenced their decision to try to avoid a repetition by using helium instead of hydrogen. These days most people know the gas from party balloons that when released float effortlessly to the ceiling – and, of course, can be used to make voices sound funny. It is the second lightest element, but a given volume of helium is twice as heavy as the same volume of hydrogen. As a result, an airship filled with helium either has to carry a much smaller load than one of the same size filled with hydrogen or has to be made far bigger. But the great advantage that helium has is that it is an inert gas and cannot catch fire. The US navy was not intending to go into the passenger carrying business, so their choice made a great deal of sense. The decision was based in part on successful helium tests with a dirigible.

The new ship was named *Shenandoah*, an Indian word meaning 'daughter of the stars'. She was not a large craft by the standard of airships of the time, with a capacity of 2,115,174 cu. ft. but helium was very expensive. She was originally powered by six Packard engines but one was later removed. The maiden flight on 4 September 1923 was the very first by a rigid frame helium airship and the crew had to learn new techniques for handling the craft. Because the gas was so expensive, valving had to be kept to a minimum and, unlike hydrogen craft, it was not fully inflated at take-off to allow room for expansion. The ship performed well but nearly came to a catastrophic end on 16 January 1924 when moored to the mast at her base at Lakehurst, New Jersey. Caught in a violent

The wreck of the *Roma* that crashed in America in February 1922.

storm the ship was ripped free and began heading straight for a group of trees. The skeleton crew on board took immediate action, throwing out a great quantities of ballast, just enough to lift it clear. After that the damaged craft was brought gingerly down to land.

After repairs were completed, the command passed to Commander Zachary Lansdowne, who had travelled as an observer on the famous Atlantic flight of *R34*. In October 1924 she went on a lengthy trip across the United States, from her base at Lakehurst to San Diego, then up the west coast to Seattle before returning to base. It was a trip that raised a lot of enthusiasm among Americans for airship travel. On later flights, Lansdowne mastered many new methods of making his airship more useful, including a demonstration of how it could be used at sea for long periods of time by being accompanied by a suitable support vessel. He managed to moor the airship to a mast on the USS *Patoka* out at sea. But all this early enthusiasm was soon to be dashed.

On 3 September 1925, the airship ran into a violent storm over Ohio. An up draught sent it shooting up at a rate of over 1000 feet a minute and buffeted by winds the strain proved too great. The ship split. The stern section fell away, carrying with it two of the engine cars and their crews, who fell to their death. The control car was the next section to fall away, carrying Cdr. Lansdowne and five of his crew. The remaining section somehow stayed aloft, and the Navigator, Charles Rosendahl, took charge and by valving helium and throwing out any heavy objects they managed to control the stricken craft, much as they would a balloon, and brought it safely to earth. Rosendahl and six others survived. The American navy continued using airships and were to build five rigid frame ships which continued in use until 1935 when the *Macon* was destroyed in a storm. But the stricken ship was able to make an emergency landing on the sea and of the 83-man crew only two were killed, the remainder being able to take to life rafts. But, as in Britain, it was the earlier tragedy that acted as a disincentive to develop civilian passenger airships.

A similar story could be told of the other European countries that continued with airship development after the end of the war. The French had acquired three Zeppelins as their share of the war loot: one of which was broken up; one was used as a training ship; and the third, *L72*, became the naval survey airship *Dixnude*. For a time, she had a very successful career, including setting a new record for endurance when she stayed up for 118 hours. Just three months later, in December 1923, she set off from her base near Toulon for a flight to Algeria, from where it was intended to make a number of surveying flights over the Sahara. She had a crew of 52, commanded by the very impressively named Lieutenant de Vaisseau du Plessis de Grenedan. He was well into the flight over the Mediterranean when he received a wireless message that informed him of a violent storm immediately ahead. He altered course to try and avoid it but at 2 a.m. on 21 December he reported that he had been unable to avoid the gale that was now lashing at his craft. The ship battled on but at 3.30 p.m. a message was received back at base to inform them that de Grenadan was going to attempt an emergency landing. That was the last message that was ever heard.

A huge search operation was mounted over the sea and the North African coast, but no sign of the airship was ever seen. Then some Sicilian fishermen recovered a body that turned out to be de Grenadan, the only one of the crew that was ever found. It was yet another discouraging airship disaster that brought all ideas of development in France to a halt.

The other country that received German Zeppelins was Italy and they also took the post war passenger ship *Bodensee*. On the delivery flight from Germany she carried two extra passengers; a German clerk and an American cinematographer had both managed to sneak on board for the ride. Although a few flights were made, there appear to have been no attempts at making a commercial success of the ship. Meanwhile the Italians had received an order for an airship, the *Roma*, from the American army. Designed by Celestino Usueli it was a semi-rigid, with a long, deep keel containing the control cabin. It was divided into sections that were shipped to America for assembly. She was originally powered by six Ansaldo engines but the American engineers were unimpressed and substituted two of them for more powerful Liberties, before the first flight. It was not an outstanding success, as all the Italian engines packed up in flight, so that the craft returned powered only by the two Liberties. After that the rest of the engines were also replaced. The suggestion was later made that this might not have been wise as the new engines were far more powerful than anything the frame had been designed to take. Whether this was a factor or not, the *Roma* came to grief on a test flight on 21 February 1922.

The flight began well enough, but then the crew noticed that the top of the envelope was beginning to flatten and there seemed to be another problem with the rudder at the tail. The ship began to head towards the earth at an angle of 45°. The captain tried to make an emergency landing on the Norfolk Country Club golf course, but as the craft approached it brushed high voltage power lines, there was a spark and in seconds *Roma* had crashed in flames. Shortly afterwards a Pathé film crew flew over the site and the film can still be seen. It is an extraordinary sight, just one mass of twisted metal. It seems amazing that anyone could survive such a disaster, yet eleven of the forty five on board did, though all were seriously injured. It seemed that, whether in Europe or America, airship development was being haunted by disasters that threatened the whole development programme.

CHAPTER TWELVE

The Polar Flights

Dreams of establishing regular passenger services may have been put on hold but there were adventurous spirits who saw other uses for airships. The lure of being the first to fly across the North Pole had never completely died away, in spite of the disastrous attempt to do so by balloon. Among the greatest enthusiasts for the idea was the Norwegian explorer, Roald Amundsen, already famous for beating Captain Scott to become the first to reach the South Pole. The original idea had been to cross the Arctic using flying boats and the expedition was planned with his fellow Norwegian, Major General Riiser-Larsen. The latter had, as mentioned earlier, trained as an airship pilot in Britain. He had heard stories about a proposed airship passenger route to link Scandinavia to London. He was aware that Oslo was, in many people's eyes, the least important

Roald Amundsen beside the seaplane in which he had hoped to make his first flight across the Arctic; he went on to be one of the two leaders of the successful airship crossing.

of the Scandinavian capitals, so he felt that a Norwegian needed to have experience of airships to make a case for inclusion. As no firm plans were emerging, he became involved with the Amundsen plans instead.

The first attempt, in 1923, never got under way, simply because the Junkers plane intended for the expedition failed to survive its test flight. For the next attempt in 1925, two Dornier Wal flying boats were shipped in sections to Spitzbergen and reassembled. In May 1925 the two aircraft took off, one of which was piloted by Riiser-Larsen, and landed on the sea, but one was too badly damaged to take off again and was abandoned; the other returned to base. It was time for a change in tactics. After the failure of the flying boat expedition, Riiser-Larsen spent some time at an aircraft factory in Italy. It was while he was there that he met the airship designer Umberto Nobile and discovered that his semi-rigid ship *N1* might be made available for a Polar expedition. There was a political problem, however, in that Mussolini was now in power and it looked very much as if the scenario played out when Zeppelin attempted to be the first to cross the Atlantic would be enacted again. The dictator did not want a Norwegian expedition to have the glory that should, he felt, go to Italy. Eventually a compromise was reached; although Amundsen would head the expedition, Nobile would be in charge of the actual flight. Amundsen and Nobile were both prickly characters and there was inevitable tension between them, neither wishing the other to have too many of the accolades should the expedition succeed. In fact, there was only one qualified airship pilot among them and that was Riiser-Larsen. The other problem was raising the money and in the event it was wealthy American, Lincoln Ellsworth, who came up with the majority of the funds. Ellsworth had been with Amundsen on the earlier attempt and now he persuaded his father to put up $100,000 to finance the attempt by airship. That is roughly a million and a half dollars at today's valuation. With the money secured, the expedition could get under way.

The seaplanes had been sent by sea but there was no question of dismantling the airship so it had to be flown from Italy to Spitzbergen. In March 1926, the *N1* was handed over flying the Italian flag; that was lowered, the Norwegian flag raised in its place and the ship rechristened *Norge*. On 10 April they left Italy to head for their first stopping off place, Pulham in Norfolk. The piloting duties were shared between Riiser-Larsen and Nobile, though the former was also responsible for navigation. That presented something of a problem. The first leg proved simple enough, flying to the base at Pulham in England. The next leg to Norway turned out to be more problematical. The most efficient cruising speed, in terms of fuel conservation, was a modest 80 km. per hour, but that could only be achieved by closing down one of the three engines. There were two amidships and one astern. The usual practice was to shut down the starboard engine which meant that there was a tendency for the port engine to drive the ship to starboard. The coxswain had to compensate for this starboard drift but when Riiser-Larsen managed to get a brief period of sleep, he found that they were well off course. Corrections were hurriedly made and they arrived safely and then headed for Oslo, where they were greeted by the king of Norway. The navigation problems continued to plague them.

Riiser-Larsen now set course for Finland but during the next stage of the flight they were plagued by clouds and fog and were unable to get a wireless bearing. He thought they were over Finland, but wasn't at all sure, so when they reached a railway line they simply followed it until they saw a station then dropped down low enough to read the name. It was called Varga, but Finnish towns had changed their names after the country gained independence and it didn't appear on the older maps. Fortunately, he had acquired a more modern version and discovered that they were between Estonia and Russia. Now that they knew where they were, they were able to set a course for their next stop at Gatchina near St. Petersburg. They had to wait there some time as work was still going on to build the temporary hangar that would be needed. Eventually they got under way again and after one more stop at Vadsö they reached Kongsfjord (King's Bay) Spitzbergen. Reading Riiser-Larsen's own account of this journey that was made just to reach the start of the actual Polar flight reminds one of just how problematic navigation still was in those days even when flying over populated areas – and emphasises the difficulties they would face crossing the Arctic where as he himself reported the view was of 'ice, ice and still more ice'.

On their arrival at King's Bay they found that they were not the first to arrive at the base. Commander Richard Byrd was already there with his Fokker plane and his pilot Floyd Bennet. He too was planning a flight over the North Pole but had a problem with the ski attachments that needed to be fixed before he could take off.

He asked if he might borrow one of the airship's mechanics to help fix it, and Riiser-Larsen suggested to Amundsen that they should let Bernt Balchen do the work. When that was agreed, the skis were fixed and Byrd set off to become the first to fly across the Pole. It has been suggested that Amundsen was furious at losing the chance to gain that honour, yet according to the first-hand account, he was happy to help set Byrd on his way. They needed to change one of the engines on the airship and Riiser-Larsen recorded that Amundsen was in no hurry to get the work done to beat Byrd to the Pole – 'Amundsen's objective was after all what lay on the other side of the Pole'.

At 9.55 on the morning of 9 May 1926, the *Norge* took off and headed north. With no landmarks to guide them, Riiser-Larsen who was in charge of navigation had to rely on two sets of measurements: the direction from which he was receiving radio signals from Kongsfjord and sightings of the sun's altitude above the horizon using a bubble sextant, which would give him a measure of the latitude. It was his job to calculate exactly when they were over the Pole. He was able to estimate the time of arrival and when the sun was at a specific height above the horizon he would know they had reached their objective. The sun was low, so he was able to observe it from the control car. He then set his sextant to the calculated altitude and waited for the sun and the bubble in his sextant to come together. At precisely 01.30 hours they were over the Pole. Amundsen dropped a Norwegian flag, Ellsworth the Stars and Stripes and Nobile the Italian flag. Riiser-Larsen ordered the coxswain to turn the ship hard left and they completed a circle of the earth in two minutes. If nothing else, they could claim to be the first to circumnavigate the globe by air. Now they set course for Alaska.

They were heading off into unknown territory and Riiser-Larsen kept regular checks on their progress. When the sun was low it was an easy matter to check their progress. He simply selected an obvious icy hummock and used a stop-watch to time how long it took for the shadow of the airship to cross it. Knowing the length of the ship, the calculation of the speed over the ground was straightforward. Checking the drift, the difference between the compass reading and the actual direction in which the ship was heading was more complex, relying mainly on the radio beacon and solar measurements to fix the position at any one time. Then the fog came down and he had to rely on weather reports of wind speed and direction to plot the course.

Their greatest problem was with ice. Not very much formed on the envelope itself, but it clung to the metal sections until bits began to break off. When that happened there was a loud bang, like a gun being fired and particles of ice shot away, some of them making holes in the envelope. Fortunately, they were only in the underside. The job of mending the holes went to a crewman, Renato Alessandrini, selected by Nobile. Riiser-Larsen was amazed by his agility at clambering all over the airship and decided he 'must have been a circus acrobat in his youth'. It was a nervous time for everyone, for if the flying ice had punctured the upper part of the envelope, nothing could have prevented the gas from escaping and they would have been forced down in the icy waste.

There were anxious times as conditions made it impossible to get a latitude bearing and Riiser-Larsen had to rely on his reckoning to plot a course and to estimate when they would reach land. Eventually it was sighted and they passed over a small settlement that Amundsen identified as Wainwright on the Alaskan coast. They now set course to fly down the Bering Straits. Then new problems overtook them. They flew into low clouds that cut out all sightings of land, and they were flying blind through the narrow straits, bordered by high mountains. It was a situation that was so dangerous that their only option was to climb above the clouds. Now they were out in the sunshine, Riiser-Larsen could again take his sextant measurements, but now the sun was high and hidden from view for an observer in the gondola. So he had to clamber up a ladder set inside what he described as an elongated sausage inside the envelope to take his measurement, then climb back down again for his calculations. He was exhausted. The flight had already lasted for 70 hours and on the first day when they were in the fog,

The *Norge* that became the first airship to fly across the North Pole.

he had managed to snatch a half hour of sleep and for the last 24 hours none at all. He was so tired he couldn't even trust himself to get his calculations right and had to ask other crew members to check them for him. To everyone's relief the calculations showed that they were heading straight down the middle of the Bering Straits, well clear of the peaks to either side. They still, however, did not know exactly where they were along that line, and coming down through the clouds to check carried its own risks. The altimeter was calibrated in terms of atmospheric pressure but with no knowledge of what the pressure was at ground level there was no way of knowing whether or not it was accurate. The crew were nervous and the tension got to Nobile's fox terrier that he'd brought along for the ride. It now began running up and down the gondola howling miserably, which did nothing to improve the mood of the crew. However, they came down low and at last sighted land, but had little idea still as to where exactly they were.

Riiser-Larsen looked down and was convinced he saw a whole troop of cavalry on the beach, who would be sure to help them land. But when he looked a second time they had gone. They were no more than an hallucination, based on his exhausted state. They were discussing how they could possibly make a safe landing, when miraculously it seemed the wind dropped and a dead calm descended. The bow rope was thrown out and several Inuit appeared and grabbed it, without realising the danger they were in: a sudden gust of wind could have taken the ship skywards and them with it. Riiser-Larsen shouted to them to let go without thinking where they were and considering that it was unlikely that anyone on the ground spoke Norwegian. But, incredibly there was a Norwegian lady among the group. Nobile set the ship down, gas was let out and all landed safely. Amundsen had achieved his goal of traversing the entire Polar Sea. They had travelled three thousand miles and had ended their epic voyage at Teller, Alaska, just 35 miles from the base at Nome, where they had hoped to finish their flight.

The expedition had been a triumph for all concerned and could not have succeeded without a brilliant and disciplined team working together. But when it was all over there was an unseemly quarrel between Amundsen and Nobile as to who deserved the most credit as leader of the expedition. As a result, when Nobile returned to Italy, he was determined to mount an expedition of his own for which he could claim undisputed leadership. The state refused to back the project, possibly because Nobile was being treated as a national hero and for Mussolini the country only had room for one such hero. However, his home city of Milan helped finance the construction of a new airship, named almost inevitably, *Italia*. As with the *Norge*, just getting to the starting point at Spitzbergen proved a trial. The ship left Italy on 15 April 1928 with eighteen on board, not counting Nobile's pet dog, heading for Stolp in northern Germany. They hit just about every conceivable type of bad weather imaginable: rain, sleet, hail and snow battered the craft carried on high winds with lightning flashing around them. After 26 hours they made it safely down to Stolp for repairs to a damaged fin. The next day they set off again in a strong north wind but made it safely to Vadsö. The final leg went well until they reached King's Bay, where they met violent winds and driving snow. They were prepared to cruise around the area until conditions settled but the ground crew radioed that conditions at ground level were favourable and they were able to come into land. It was still blowing hard, and too windy for the crew to risk towing the ship into the hangar, so it was left moored to the mast with a watch on duty to make sure there were no problems. One of the three engines had developed a fault during the approach and had to be replaced. This was not intended to be a one-off epic flight, but rather a whole series of flights, including flying over King Nicholas II Land (Severneya Zenya) an archipelago in the Russian Arctic, exploring unknown regions of Greenland and, of course, a flight over the Pole.

The first flight started out on 11 May but was soon forced back by the weather. The exposed ship was covered with snow that built up, creating a real threat as it weighed down on the structure. But a thaw set in, all was back to normal and preparations were made for the next flight. This was a survey flight and in spite of occasional bad weather, including patches of fog and occasional snowstorms, they were able to remain flying for 69 hours, covering over 15,000 square miles of territory, much of it never previously explored. During the periods of fine weather, the crew took some excellent photos of the terrain. It was an undoubted triumph and a superb demonstration of the value of the airship in conducting surveys that would have been difficult if not impossible by any other means.

The flight to the Pole set off on 29 May. With a strong tail wind, the Pole was reached after just 19 hours flying time and the usual ceremonies were performed; the Italian and Milanese flags were dropped, together with a wooden cross presented by the Pope

The *Italia* in the Arctic.

and a religious medal. There had been some thought of dropping a party down onto the ice by a winch, together with an inflatable raft and supplies. In the event, the wind was simply too strong and they headed for home. There may have been some disappointment at not being able to make the drop to the surface but in the event it proved to be a life-saving stroke of good fortune. It was to be the only lucky chance that the expedition would enjoy. In spite of now having to return in the face of the powerful wind that had bowled them along so easily, Nobile decided to make the journey back to Spitzbergen, instead of continuing towards Alaska with the wind behind him.

Progress was painfully slow, and although they received regular radio reports that the weather ahead was better and calmer they never seemed to be reaching the easy passage that would take them safely home. Conditions were bad and, just as it had with the *Norge,* ice formed on metal structures and again was shot off into the envelope and once again Alessandrini was on board to carry out running repairs. Navigation was a major problem; compass readings near the magnetic North Pole are hopelessly unreliable and Nobile had to rely on dead reckoning, estimating his own speed and direction of travel and taking account of the likely wind speed and direction. When he finally arrived at what he thought was a reasonably accurate fix on the airship's position, he was actually in error by a massive 350 miles. The situation was now so serious that the wireless operator sent out a message to say that if they radioed him and received no answer 'I have a good reason'.

The first sign of a really serious problem came when the elevator control jammed when the ship was travelling at just 1,000 ft. above the ice. The engines were cut and she rose into sunlight at a height of 3,000 ft. while the elevator mechanism was freed. An hour later at 10.25 a.m. on 25 May, the ship suddenly appeared to have become tail heavy and was falling steadily. Nobile ordered engines to be turned to full power and sent Allessandrini into the tail section to check the gas valves. It was all too late and Nobile ordered all electrical equipment to be switched off. He knew now that a crash was inevitable and the last thing they wanted was a spark to set everything ablaze. Minutes later the control cabin hit the ground, splitting apart and Nobile was hurled onto the ice, together with eight of the crew. With the sudden loss of weight, the rest of the airship rose again with six men still on board. The Chief Engineer, Ettore Arduino, began hurling out emergency supplies, together with the life raft that had been intended for use at the Pole. But soon, the powerless, unsteerable remains of *Italia* were floating off into the distance. Neither it nor the men on board were ever found, and among those who lost their lives was the agile Allessadrini.

Those on the ground suffered a variety of injuries. Nobile had a head wound, broken arm, broken leg and a cracked rib. Four of the survivors were more or less uninjured and on their feet – Mariano, Behounek, Trojani and Viglieri – while the radio operator, Biagi, was only badly winded, as he had grasped the portable radio when the crash was inevitable and was still stuck in the wreck. Cecioni had broken both legs, Malmgrem had a badly injured shoulder, while Zappi had suspected broken ribs. Pomella had apparently survived the crash but died shortly afterwards. The survivors now began to assess their situation. Within the wreckage they found food including chocolate and pemmican, a flare gun, a revolver with ammunition and silk from which they could erect a tent for cover. There were sleeping bags, and Nobile was made as comfortable as possible, wrapped in a bag for warmth. Meanwhile Biagi had been able to fabricate an antenna and was sending out an SOS.

The following day they searched the wreckage to see what could be salvaged and found more food supplies. They then had to work out how to ration it out and estimate the maximum time that might elapse before they were discovered. They allowed for a twenty five day wait, which meant each man could have an allowance of 300 grams per day, scarcely a feast but enough to survive. A polar bear appeared and headed towards the makeshift camp. Malmgren shot it and the party enjoyed the luxury of fresh meat for a time. Attempts to contact the base ship *Citta di Milano* were frustratingly unsuccessful, largely because the radio operators on board were not listening out but were busy sending out inconsequential messages of their own. The SOS signals were eventually picked up by an amateur radio enthusiast in Russia and a rescue operation was then mounted. It was thoroughly badly co-ordinated. The captain of the *Citta di Milano* was unwilling to take any actions of his own and kept telegraphing Rome for instructions. Men who knew the region at once volunteered to help: Amundsen, in spite of his earlier feud with Nobile, offered his services, but the Italian government rebuffed him. They did, however, accept the assistance of Riiser-Larsen and Nobile's other former colleague Ellsworth offered to help finance a search party. The Italian government was asked to send planes to the area but refused, and it was only when a friend of Nobile's Arturo Mercanti told them he would hire private planes himself that they were shamed into sending two sea planes to the area.

Out on the ice, three of the survivors decided they would trek across the ice to try to get to some form of habitation to find help. Along the way, Malmgren collapsed and insisted that the others went on without him. They had no choice and left him to die alone. They were eventually rescued by a Russian ice-breaker on 12 July. Meanwhile the situation for those left behind improved enormously when they were seen by a spotter plane, which dropped them supplies on 23 June. The following day Captain Lundborg landed his De Havilland Moth plane at the site and took off with the injured Nobile and his terrier, which had survived without any injuries whatsoever. He returned the same day but suffered engine failure and was himself stuck on the ice. By early July all had been brought back to safety.

The Italian government had never shown any enthusiasm for the expedition and had been equally unenthusiastic about the rescue; now they were inclined to blame Nobile for the disaster. It seemed that the popular hero was about to become the unpopular villain. But when the survivors returned to Italy they received a rapturous reception from the general public. Nobile, however, was so disgusted by the experience that he left the country to become director of airship research in the Soviet Union. The *Italia* had demonstrated the immense value of the airship for surveying, had shown endurance that would allow it to cover thousands of miles and had eventually only come to grief because of the harsh Arctic conditions. In spite of these facts it was still decided that Italy would build no more airships. Other countries, however, still saw a great potential and set about realising it.

Chapter Thirteen

Flying the Atlantic

Airship design had improved immensely in the years following the end of the Great War and the Zeppelin Company began to have ambitious plans for starting a passenger service, linking Europe to America. There were several reasons why that was a potentially profitable idea. In the 1920s, virtually the only way to cross the Atlantic was by ship. Looking back on those days of the great ocean-going liners, it seems almost unbelievably romantic. The images we have are of luxurious accommodation and magnificent décor – and each vessel had its own style, from chic Art Deco modernism to passenger lounges that looked more like the oak panelled rooms of a London club for gentlemen. As well as luxurious comfort, the liners hired the finest chefs to produce tempting menus. None of this, of course, applied to the poorest passengers in steerage. But even if you were a first-class passenger, there was one factor that could not be ignored – the Atlantic Ocean itself. Many years ago, I made an Atlantic crossing in a Cunard liner and it was fine while the weather was good, but when the swell rose and the waters were breaking over the bows, it was very noticeable that there were more and more empty tables at mealtimes. The airship not only offered an alternative, it also reduced the travelling time.

Hugo Eckener who was now the company chairman, made a careful study of how an airship could compete and what design features it needed to have to make it viable and profitable. The first advantage was, he felt, relative speeds. The record for an Atlantic crossing by sea was still held by the *Mauretania* with an average speed of just under 25 knots (27 mph) a record established in 1909 that had remained unchallenged for almost two decades. The airships could easily surpass this. The other factors he had to consider were size, reliability and safety. The craft would have to be big enough to take sufficient paying passengers to make a profit. Reliability was obviously important if they were to run a scheduled service. In spite of a variety of accidents involving airships, Eckener was satisfied that overall safety would not be a problem. He envisaged a craft in which there would be a large number of gas bags with a mixture of hydrogen and helium to reduce the fire risk.

As an extra precaution he suggested moving from petrol to diesel engines; the heavier oil being far less likely to ignite. He was sure that a flight would in general be a lot more comfortable than a sea voyage and saw no difficulty in attracting passengers; some attracted by the shorter crossing time and others, at first, enjoying the social cache of being among the few able to boast of having flown the Atlantic.

One of the luxurious cabins on the *Graf Zeppelin*.

Eckener went on to produce detailed financial assessments. He thought that to start the service there would need to be three Zeppelins and a one-off capital cost to provide the necessary facilities at either end, such as hangars and mooring masts. The capital outlay was estimated at 35 million marks. With an airship carrying 30 passengers paying 2,500 marks each for a single ticket, together with income from mail and other freight, there would be a profit of 234,000 marks per round trip. And as there were plans for each craft to make 50 round trips per annum that was a very healthy return on the initial investment. There was only one obvious problem looming up ahead – competition from aircraft. On 21 May 1927, Charles Lindbergh completed his famous non-stop flight from New York to Paris. He made the crossing in a single-seat monoplane but it must have been obvious to aviation experts everywhere that it was only a matter of time before bigger, passenger-carrying planes were making the same journey. Eckener, however, was confident that that day was far enough away to make the airship viable for years to come.

Eckener had understood that size was important but for the first of the new craft construction was limited by the size of hangar then available at Friedrichshafen. Nevertheless, the new craft *LZ127* was impressive enough at 776 ft. long and 100 ft. diameter with a capacity of 2,650,000 cu. ft. Even so it was not able to carry Eckener's ideal complement of passengers, being limited to just twenty. On 8 July 1928 the new ship was christened the *Graf Zeppelin* after the company's founder and the ceremony was conducted by his daughter. Unlike the earlier generation of passenger airships, the new vessel was designed with comfort very much in mind. The cabins were both luxurious and rather homely, while the day area was equipped with comfortable tables and chairs and a promenade area with windows from which the passengers could enjoy the view. These extended along the side of the day cabin, with angled glass providing an excellent view down to the ground. It was probably worth the high price of the tickets for that view, especially when flying over the unique cityscape of Manhattan.

The maiden flight set off on 18 September and lasted for 35 hours, going out over the North Sea and returning with a flight over Berlin. Altogether there were five test flights made to test the airship's performance and on the last of these as it crossed over Berlin, a bouquet of flowers was dropped by parachute into the garden of the Palace where President Von Hindenburg was celebrating his

81st birthday. All went well and the first Atlantic flight was planned for 10ᵗʰ October, Columbus Day in America. It was a splendid way to get publicity – marking the European discovery of the New World. Unforttunately, the weather refused to co-operate. When the day arrived, the Atlantic was being battered by ferocious gales that had many ships in serious trouble. However, it was only necessary to defer the take-off by twenty-four hours. But there did have to be a change of plan. The original idea was to have followed the usual shipping route, but that would have taken the airship into the dangerous conditions still prevailing in mid-Atlantic. Two routes were considered; the northerly one via Scotland and Iceland or a southerly route via Gibraltar and Bermuda. The latter was selected. They set off with thirty-seven crew and twenty passengers, including big wigs from the Air Ministry and six correspondents from leading newspapers, at 7.30 a.m.

At first, everything went well and in perfect conditions the passengers were treated to magnificent views of the Alps and the vineyards of Burgundy, and by evening they saw the lights of Barcelona. The conditions seemed perfect as they headed off towards Madeira, but then they received the weather reports that suggested that they would be running into the edge of the storm that had delayed them in the first place. Sure enough, they were soon in the dark clouds, illuminated from time to time by streaks of lightning. As they hit winds estimated at around 75 knots, the craft began to pitch alarmingly but as the engines were throttled back to half power, the journey became a lot more stable. Even so, they stayed with the storm for some time and when they finally emerged into the sunshine, the crew reported that there was some damage to the port fin. As it was in danger of affecting the elevator controls, the only solution wa to attempt repairs in mid-air. And crew members crawled out onto the fabric to make everything safe and sound again.

There were more squalls over Bermuda, but the ship sailed on and at 10 a.m. on 15 October crossed the American coast, heading for Washington. After flying low over the city, the ship carried on with the final leg to the Lakehurst base, docking after a total flight time of 111 hours 43 minutes to the acclaim of a huge crowd, estimated to be around 20,000. For the return journey, Eckener decided to take the northern route. This time, as well as the passengers, he had a hundred thousand letters and postcards. The weather was, if anything, worse than that encountered on the outward flight.

The *Graf* Zeppelin taking off.

First, they ran into squally winds and rain, then into a dense wall of fog, so deep they were unable to safely climb above it. They were, in effect, flying blind, with no means of checking their position. When the fog eventually cleared, they discovered they had been blown off course by a staggering 300 miles and were actually flying over Newfoundland. They were at last able to get a fix on their position and chart a new course for Europe. They were hampered by fog once again at the end of the journey but made it back to base shortly before dawn. Eckener stood off until first light at 7 a.m. having achieved a new record for transatlantic crossings of 71 hours and 7 minutes.

Although the flight attracted immense publicity and was generally considered a triumph, it had yet to achieve its main function: there was no rush of investors. The German government seemed reluctant to take an interest in the project and private finance was equally unforthcoming. Eckener decided that he needed another publicity flight, one that would give the passengers a chance to view some of the finest scenery and historic sites that Europe and the Mediterranean countries had to offer. But, once again, he was held up by an unusually bad winter. They eventually got under way with a suitably impressive array of VIPs for a cruise that anyone would envy even today, when air travel is a commonplace. They cruised low over the Riviera and passed out over Elba and Corsica, heading for Italy. Reaching Rome they flew low over the city, giving the passengers a wonderful view of the Vatican and the Forum and Coliseum. Then they headed south, passing over Cyprus and Crete for another breathtaking close up of the ancient city of Jerusalem. There was a little surprise for the guests as Eckener brought the ship down low across the Dead Sea, so that he could inform them they had unique experience of flying below sea level. Ideally the next sensational view would have been the Pyramids, but they were forbidden to fly over Egypt. They did, however, reach Athens at dawn as they headed for home. There was to be one last piece of drama as Eckener took the craft to an altitude of 6,500 feet to cross the Alps. If that trip hadn't impressed the VIPs then nothing would. But even so, Eckener planned an even more ambitious venture: he would fly right round the world. An appeal was made to fund the expedition and money poured in from an enthusiastic public.

On 1 August, the *Graf Zeppelin* set off to the American base at Lakehurst to collect the passengers who had been invited on the epic flight. Once they were aboard, there was a by now almost familiar flight back to Freidrichshafen. The next leg was certainly not routine. This was a flight over what was literally in some parts, uncharted territory. They flew out across the Soviet Union and the vast wastes of Siberia but ahead of them lay the Stanovoi range of mountains. They had been told by a Soviet officer that the peaks rose up to 6,000 ft. but if they followed the valley of the River Vi they would reach a pass at a level of 3,300 ft. It turned out that the pass was higher than anticipated but the valley became so narrow that there was no possibility of turning round and retreating. The mountains rose on either side as they skimmed over the pass and an American admiral on board asked nonchalantly if they were supposed to be picking buttercups. It was with great relief that they emerged just as dusk was about to fall and they could head out across the Sea of Japan. It had been a perilous passage but the ship had made it safely and they landed in Tokyo, having covered 7,000 miles in 101 hours. The next leg would take them to the west coast of America, but the passage was shrouded in cloud and fog, and it must have been a considerable relief when the fog cleared and the familiar landmark of San Francisco's Golden Gate Bridge came into view. They flew on down the coast for a landing in Los Angeles, having clocked up another 79 hours of flying time. Now all that remained was the last leg, back to Lakehurst, which they reached without mishap. Altogether they had flown 21,250 miles.

The *Graf Zeppelin* was to make many more memorable flights and in a long career that lasted right up to 1937, she made 505 flights covering more than a million miles. Throughout her time in service there were surprisingly few technical difficulties; there was, however, a major political problem. When Hitler came to power a decree went out that the airship would in future be emblazoned with the swastika, emblem of the Nazi party. Eckener simply refused to obey the command and the insignia never appeared. His fate could have been sealed, but the worst that happened was a demand from the Fuhrer that his name should never again be given any publicity. Eckener survived the Second World War and was one of those who pressed for Franco-German co-operation to repair the ravages of the past. He was briefly involved with Goodyear in a post-war plan to build a new design of rigid airship, but the plans came to nothing. He died in 1954 at the age of 86 and will be remembered as one of the great airship pioneers.

The *Graf Zeppelin* being welcomed home after the epic flight round the world.

If the German government had proved reluctant to invest in airship development, the British were equally lethargic. In 1924, the government finally agreed to put in hand a research programme at a cost of £1,350,000 spread over three years. The idea was to provide an air service that would link Britain to the Empire, with flights to Africa, India and Canada. Two experimental craft were to be built, with a new numbering system: they would be *R100* and *R101*.

The work was to be the responsibility of two organisations. The Airship Guarantee Company was a subsidiary of Vickers, headed by Commander Dennis Burney, a great enthusiast of airship development, while the technical design team was led by Dr Barnes Wallis. The other organisation involved was the official Air Ministry team based at Cardington. The government laid down specific criteria that the design teams had to meet. The airship was to have a capacity of five million cu. ft. with a gross lift of 150 tons, while the overall weight, excluding fuel must not exceed 90 tons. Top speed had to be at least 70 mph, with a cruising speed of 65 mph when fully loaded and, in light of the failures that had led to the tragic loss of *R38*, rigorous standards were imposed for testing stress factors.

The Cardington team began work on the *R101*. It was to have many design features that were very different from earlier versions of British airships and the initial tests were carried out using models, tested in the wind tunnel at the National Physics Laboratory. Once these had proved satisfactory, the older airships *R33* and *R36* were adapted and subjected to rigorous tests on the ground. They were not, however, tested in flight. A section of the proposed airship was constructed and tested to destruction. The results of all these tests were passed to the other team. Among the new features that were specially designed were the diesel engines, which Eckener had earlier recommended for Zeppelins, as being safer than petrol. There was, however, a problem; the diesels were heavier than petrol engines of the same power. To keep within the weight restrictions imposed by the government, they were limited in the size of engine and as a result they were never quite able to reach the 700 horse power output that had also been specified. The Vickers team realised there was an insoluble problem and settled for lighter petrol engines.

The *R101* was completed first and began her test flights on 14 October 1929. There were technical problems, the most serious of which occurred during rough weather when it was discovered the internal gas bags were moving from side to side, and catching on protruding parts of the frame, such as nuts, resulting in tears and leaking gas. Instead of attempting to redesign the arrangements, it was decided that the problem could be solved more easily – and more cheaply – by simply adding extra padding. There was a lot of pressure on the Vickers team as by this time the *R100* had also been completed and was performing well. The *R101* however continued to have problems with the gas bags and they were not getting the required lift, so changes had to be made that included altering the passenger accommodation, rewiring the gas bags and introducing a new middle section and extra gas bag. In order to promote the airship, the team had planned a trip to India, but before that they were due to make an appearance at the Hendon Air Show. For the crowd it was a magnificent spectacle as the elegant, long ship passed low overhead. For the crew it was a nightmare as they seemed to be losing gas and could barely keep airborne. Back at base, it was discovered that there were two problems. The cheap solution of adding padding had simply not worked and gas was escaping through the valves. It was now clear that serious remedial work was needed before any trip to India could even be contemplated.

In an ideal world, this work would have been carried out calmly and thoroughly, but they received a message from the Air Minister, Lord Thomson, to say that he had political meetings in September and he insisted that the airship should take him there. With the best will in the world, the team were quite unable to get the ship ready on time, but they promised a date in October, which annoyed the Minister, but there was nothing he could do to change the situation. The work was completed and the ship undertook a test flight, but the conditions were good – not at all like those that had revealed the problems. Nevertheless, it was decided to go ahead with the Indian flight, though there was one major obstacle to overcome. In order to receive its airworthiness certificate, the airship should have undergone speed trials, but these had not taken place. It looked as if there would be yet more delays and the Director of Airship Development wrote to Lord Thomson to say that he was not happy that the ship had been thoroughly tested and that it was too soon to attempt the difficult flight to India. The Minister would brook no further delays and orders were given to issue a temporary certificate that would be ratified once the necessary speed tests had been carried out during the journey.

On the evening of 4 October 1930, *R101* set off on the first leg of her flight to India, with Lord Thomson, who must have been delighted to have got his way, and Sir Sefton Brancker, the Director of Civil Aviation who had wanted the trip postponed and was probably feeling a good deal less sanguine. Crossing the French coast all seemed to be going well, but shortly afterwards the ship hit stormy weather. She was near Beauvais when watchers on the ground reported seeing her rolling badly, then go into a steep dive. Water ballast was released and for a moment it looked as if she was rising again, but then the nose came down and she hit a hillside and skidded to a stop. It seemed at first as if little damage had been done, but seconds later the hydrogen was ablaze and the ship destroyed. Of the fifty-four on board, only six survived, but the Minister and the Director were both killed.

This was a disaster that should never have happened. It was clear to the experts that the ship was not ready but they were forced to yield to ministerial pressure. Had all the necessary tests been carried out, no doubt suitable alterations could have been made and, if that was not possible, the design could have been abandoned in favour of the more successful *R100*. But the airship had received such huge publicity that there was no way back. *R100* was permanently grounded and eventually sold for scrap. The British airship programme was ended.

CHAPTER FOURTEEN

The End of an Era

Hugo Eckener had always been aware that the *Graf Zeppelin* fell short of his ideal airship. Zeppelin Airlines now had government support, so in 1934 plans were put in hand to build a bigger, even better airship. The threat from aircraft competition had increased, thanks to the development of a new generation of seaplanes. So one of the requirements was an increase in speed, ideally with a cruising speed of well over 80 mph To meet this demand, more powerful engines would be needed and Eckener, always very safety conscious, specified they should be diesels. He also proposed that as an extra security measure, there should be the usual gas bags of hydrogen within the craft, but that they should be surrounded by bags of helium to reduce the fire risk. The added weight of the engines and helium meant that this airship *LZ129* had to be a monster, with a capacity of just over seven million cubic feet.

The *Hindenburg* in flames: the fire spread from the tail to engulf the whole craft.

The extra size meant that the ship could offer even more luxurious accommodation than the *Graf Zeppelin*. Theoretically the airship could carry seventy passengers, but the numbers were generally kept down to fifty, so that there was the luxury of extra space for everyone, a luxury that was, of course, reflected in the ticket prices. The cabins were comparatively large and luxurious including special features, such as shower rooms. Twenty cabins also had state rooms. The public rooms were just as grand, with a splendid dining room, where food was provided by a first-rate chef and his three assistants: a smoking room and bar, a writing room and one of the rooms even had a Blüthner piano, made of specially lightweight materials so that it only weighed 50 kg. In short, the lucky passengers had the amenities that they might have expected on a luxury liner, but with one special bonus. The greatest attraction of all was certainly the 50 ft. long promenade deck with sloping windows to give views both outwards and down to the ground. Another feature that was much admired was the quietness of the airship in flight; the noise levels in the public rooms were measured to be appreciably lower than those on one of the great ocean liners. In other words, the new airship could now claim to offer the very best that travellers could expect in the early twentieth century. The Zeppelin Company were delighted with the result and felt confident that once she went into service the response would be so favourable that she would only be the first of a succession of similar airships. Today she is not remembered for her successes, but only for her ultimate failure. The new airship was christened *Hindenburg*.

The maiden flight took place on 23 March 1936 and a week later she undertook her first long distance flight to Rio de Janeiro. On the return across the Atlantic, two of the four engines cut out and although one was eventually restarted, she had run for 42 hours on just the two. On her return to Germany she was taken out of service for a month while Daimler dealt with the engine problem. When that was sorted the airship went into regular service and was so successful that it was decided to increase the passenger carrying capacity by adding twenty more cabins. By the spring of 1937, she had made ten round trips to North America and seven to Rio. Confidence was high and a new company was set up as the German-American Zeppelin Transport Company, to build more airships and extend the service as a joint venture, using both German and American ships. Then on 4 May 1937, the *Hindenburg* left Germany for what should have been another routine flight to New York.

On 6 May, the airship was over New York, giving passengers the obligatory close up view of the Empire State Building. At four o'clock that afternoon the airship had reached Lakehurst, but conditions were poor with low cloud and rain, so the Captain, Max Pruss, decided to hold off until the conditions improved. At seven there was a break in the weather and the great airship made its approach and everything went, it appeared, according to plan. Two trail ropes were dropped and attached to railway cars, running on special tracks, that then would be moved so that the airship could be safely moored. The whole process was being described on radio by Herb Morrison of WLS Chicago, who was watching from a balcony with his engineer, Charlie Nehlsen. At first, he was describing a very ordinary scene, with passengers waving from the windows. Then everything changed, and the words that followed were to be heard around the world.

'It's starting to rain again; it's … the rain had (uh) slacked up a little bit. The back motors of the ship are just holding it (uh) just enough to keep it from … It's burst into flames! Get this, Charlie; get this Charlie! It's fire …and it's crashing! It's crashing terrible! Oh, my! Get out of the way, please! It's burning and bursting into flames and the … and it's falling on the mooring mast. And all the folks agree that this is terrible; this is the worst of the worst catastrophes in the world. Oh it's …it's flames … Crashing, oh! Four- or five-hundred feet into the sky and it …it's a terrible crash, ladies and gentlemen, It's smoke and it's in flames now; and the frame is crashing to the ground, not quite to the mooring mast. Oh, the humanity! And all the passengers screaming around here. I told you; it- I can't even talk to people, their friends are on there! Ah! It's … it… it's a ah! … I can't talk ladies and gentlemen. Honest; it's just laying there a mass of smoking wreckage. Ah! I … I can't talk, ladies and gentlemen and everybody can hardly breathe and talk and the screaming. I … I …I'm sorry. Honest: I … I can hardly breathe I … I'm going to step inside, where I cannot see it. Charlie, that's terrible. Ah,.. I can't. Listen, folks: I … I'm gonna have to stop for a minute because I've lost my voice. This is the worst thing I've ever witnessed.'

The flight was also being filmed for Pathé, and today one can see the scene all over again on a computer, and watching it what is so devastatingly striking is the speed with which the disaster happened and also the bravery of those ground crew who, instead of running from the inferno, dashed towards it to help the survivors. The combination of film and commentary make this one of the most moving accounts of a disaster in aviation history.

Anyone listening in could be forgiven for thinking that everyone on board had perished but in fact Captain Pruss had made no attempt to keep the ship level. As the stern section disappeared in flames, the bows shot up with the loss of weight, and then fell back to earth. Many in the control gondola and the forward cabins managed to escape. In all 62 of the 97 aboard somehow managed to get out, though many of those were injured and suffered burns. The enquiry headed by Hugo Eckener eventually decided that there had been a leak of gas from a stern cell, which had then risen and filled the upper fin. It then appeared that it was set alight by static electricity. It was, Eckener, believed, a freak accident. *LZ130* was already in production and he suggested that it should be allowed to go into operation, but that in order to reassure the public, only helium would be used. The problem was that they needed to get the gas from America and it seemed possible that agreement would be reached. Then Hitler invaded Austria, a second European war seemed inevitable, and the export of helium was banned. The dream of a Zeppelin passenger service was ended. It did not, however, mark the end of airship development.

The Goodyear Company had been building airships for the navy since the First World War but in the 1920s they began production of comparatively small non-rigid airships for commercial use. The outbreak of war in 1939 persuaded the navy that they now had a need for crafts to patrol the Atlantic seaboard, given the threat of attacks by German submarines. There had been success in the previous world war with dirigibles and one of the early versions was officially classified as Dirigible, Type-B, limp. In the new conflict this was shortened to Blimp and the new name stuck. At first this was seen simply as a precautionary measure as the United States was still officially neutral. Then the Japanese attacked Pearl Harbor and everything changed. Production was at once stepped up and during 1942 Goodyear turned out almost a hundred K-type Blimps.

The prototype of the class *K-2* was a midget compared with the magnificent passenger Zeppelins, with a capacity of just a little over 400,000 cu. ft. But the Class was ideal for submarine patrols as they could travel slowly if needed, but fast enough with a top

A K-Class Blimp on patrol.

speed of 78 mph to turn and protect stragglers from a convoy. They could also fly quite low and hover if necessary. The forty-foot long control car had all the very latest equipment for picking up submarines: radar with a range of 90 miles; sonar buoys that could detect the underwater sounds of a submarine's engines; and up to date navigation aids for day and night flying. The craft had a machine gun for their own protection and carried six depth bombs for attack. Soon bases were established all round the American coast, and in June 1944 *K-123* and *K-130* became the first non-rigid airships to make an Atlantic crossing, when they flew to Morocco for operations in the Mediterranean.

The Blimps very rarely engaged submarines but that did certainly not mean they had no value. Quite the contrary; the general feeling was that the sight of a Blimp escorting a convoy was itself sufficient to keep the submarines at bay. The navy boasted that no ship had ever been lost to U-boats if it had been escorted by a Blimp. There was one memorable action, when *K-74* caught a U-boat on the surface just off the Florida coast. The Blimp went on the attack and the U-boat returned fire, hitting the Blimp and doing so much damage that the airship had to be ditched in the sea. The U-boat's and the Blimp's position had been relayed to the surface craft and soon the crew were picked up, apart from one unfortunate man who was attacked by a shark and killed. However, the survivors had the satisfaction of being told that the U-boat had itself now been destroyed.

The US navy Blimps were steadily reduced in number at the end of the war but they continued to play a role until the 1960s when the Airship division was finally disbanded. The age of the great passenger airships and military airships had come to an end, but that did not mean the end of the lighter than air craft. But it was not so much the airship as the 'old fashioned' balloon that was to enjoy a renaissance.

Chapter Fifteen

A New Beginning

In the last few chapters we have traced the development of balloons into steerable, powered airships and that might have given the impression that once the airship had proved successful then interest in the old-fashioned balloons had disappeared. This was not the case. People had discovered an interesting thing about balloons; flying with them was actually fun. Wealthy amateurs took to ballooning as a sport and manufacturers flourished. The first body set up to organise the sport was the Aero Club de Paris, founded in 1898. Others followed throughout Europe and America. On 4 September 1901, Frank Hodges Butler together with his daughter and the Hon, Charles Rolls, later to become famous as one half of Rolls Royce, took a balloon flight from Crystal Palace, with the professional aeronaut Stanley Spencer in charge. They stayed aloft for nearly two hours and enjoyed the experience so much that they thought it would be a good idea to set up a club for like-minded enthusiasts. The result was the formation a few days later of the Aero Club of the United Kingdom, later to become the Royal Aero Club.

One of the important functions of the new organisation was the issuing of Aeronauts' Certificates. In order to qualify, the applicant had to produce evidence that he or she had made at least twelve day ascents and one night ascent and then had made two more ascents, overseen by competent observers. If the Secretary was satisfied he would then authorise the applicant to make a solo ascent and if that was also satisfactory and the Committee approved, then the certificate was granted. Members could use the facilities of the Hurlingham Club for ascents, and the Club had its own balloons that were available for hire. These were gas balloons and a special gas main was available at the club. The average cost was nine guineas a day, around £800 at today's prices. It was not just the Aero Club that hired out balloons. One could go to a professional company such as Spencer Brothers and book oneself a ten day holiday, complete with the services of a professional aeronaut. But that would set you back well over £100. Ballooning might be described as a 'popular sport', but one had to be wealthy to enjoy it.

Ballooning was not limited to males, and in France there was a separate Stella Club for women; Mme. Surcouf, wife of the balloon designer Edouard Surcouf, had the honour of being the first woman to be awarded an Aeronauts' Certificate. Soon a variety of competitive events were being organised, such as the Hedges Butler Challenge Cup for the longest flight made in Great Britain by an amateur aeronaut. The most famous contest was for the Gordon Bennett Trophy. James Gordon Bennett was the publisher of the New York Herald who had already established a motor racing trophy and now he agreed to do the same for flight. The Trophy became best known for its latter days, when aircraft competed, but for the first event of September 1906, it was limited to balloons. In all, sixteen balloons from seven countries set off from Paris and the prize for the longest flight went to the American, Frank P. Lahm who finished up landing on the North Yorkshire Moors after a flight of 647 km. There were a number of other less demanding contests, such as 'Hare and Hounds', in which the hare set off and the prize went to whichever of the hounds could land closest to it. This was all good-natured fun, but the start of war in 1914 brought such frivolities to an end. It was to be many years before ballooning once again became a popular pastime.

In the period immediately after the end of the Second World War, most people in Britain, if they thought about balloons at all,

Ed Yost who pioneered modern ballooning with his use of synthetic materials and propane burners.

thought of the barrage balloons that for years had hovered over towns and cities. For a few scientists, however, balloons had a very different connotation. Scientists were aware that there was a lot of valuable information to be gained by studying the upper atmosphere, not least in improving the somewhat inexact science of weather forecasting. There were, however, limits beyond which, given the technology of the day, human beings could not go. In 1892, the French scientist Gustave Hermite worked with the aeronaut Georges Besançon to develop an unmanned balloon to carry instruments to previously unreached heights. Their first trials used balloons of many different sizes, with capacities varying from 1,000 to 17,500 cu. ft. and made from anything from paper to silk. The following year another Frenchman Jules Richard made an instrument-carrying balloon that ascended to 50,000 feet. These early experiments suggested that unmanned balloons had a real future in meteorology and discussions at a special conference held in Paris in 1896 led to the formation of an international programme of research.

Over the years, instrumentation was improved to produce ever more accurate readings, with much of the research being carried out for the Bosch Company by two German scientists, Richard Assmann and Arthur Berson. In 1901 they introduced rubber balloons that were designed to expand as they rose until they reached the required altitude, at which point they burst and a parachute opened up to carry the instruments safely back to earth. Over the years, bigger balloons came into use and new discoveries were made. In 1902 the meteorologist Teisserene de Bort made a discovery that revolutionised ideas about the upper atmosphere. He found a region of the upper air between 33,000 and 66,00 ft. where the temperature no longer fell and seemed even to rise slightly. He had discovered what we now know as the stratosphere. By the middle of the twentieth century, the use of balloons in meteorology and in the exploration of the limits of earth's atmosphere was very much accepted as an important tool for scientific research. One of those engaged in this work was an American, Ed Yost.

The 1950s were the years of the Cold War and mutual suspicion between the West and the Communist controlled countries of Europe. Intelligence seemed to be vital and the Americans hit on a novel idea for how they might get a spy into enemy territory entirely undetected; he would arrive via a small balloon, and once he had made a safe landing he would simply release the balloon to drift

Don Cameron with his first balloon, the *Bristol Belle*.

away on the wind. The idea was put to the leading balloon expert of the day, Ed Yost. He was interested in developing the notion, but also saw that such a balloon might have wider uses than spying. He set up a company at Sioux Falls, South Dakota, and realised that with the new technology now available, he could go back to the origins of ballooning. He would make a hot air balloon. What made the idea so attractive was the availability of new lightweight synthetic materials and an easily stored fuel in the form of propane canisters. His first balloon was made from coated nylon and in order to keep the load

A Cameron balloon manufactured for commercial advertising, and remarkably realistic in appearance – apart from being vastly bigger than an actual car.

as light as possible he replaced the usual wicker basket with a camp stool slung below the envelope. He was his own test pilot and made his first, short flight in Nebraska on 22 October 1960, when he rose to a height of 500 ft and then dropped back again. A certain amount of reorganisation was necessary before a more successful second flight was undertaken. Eventually he returned to Sioux Falls and after being told that the government were happy with his work, began developing his balloons for recreational use.

He made a number of flights in America and then decided to take his ideas to Europe. He and a colleague, Don Pickard, decided that the best way to get publicity would be a cross Channel flight. They received the backing of the French promoter Charles Dolfus, who literally showed his enthusiasm for ballooning by dropping his trousers and displaying his backside to the two Americans: on one buttock there was a tattoo of a hot air balloon and one of a gas balloon on the other. The two men flew from Rye on the south coast. The arrangement was, to say the least, somewhat precarious. Instead of the camp stool of earlier flights, the two men now sat on a plank hung from wires, with the propane cylinders beside them. When it came to landing, the idea was that they would cut two of the suspension wires so that they would skid along the ground until they ran into something, hopefully not too solid, that brought them to a halt. It did work and they ended up in a French hedge.

Yost's exploits soon attracted a great deal of media attention, and there was a big feature about him in the *National Geographic Magazine*. A copy was lying around in the bar of a gliding club, where it was picked up by a young man who had a passion for all things aeronautical. As a boy, he had made model aeroplanes and later went to university to study aeronautical engineering. He read the article, was impressed and decided to build a balloon for himself in the basement of his home in Bristol. When it was completed, he named it the *Bristol Belle* and it attracted a great deal of attention. He realised that there was a real demand for these new types of balloons and decided to set up as a manufacturer. His name was Don Cameron and today the business has long since moved out of the basement to a factory in South Bristol and Cameron Balloons now make up to a hundred balloons a year, many of them for export.

In recent years, ballooning has become ever more popular with the general public and also with commercial firms looking for a different type of advertising. Cameron Balloons began making balloons specifically designed as advertisements. At first, this was little more than adding a company logo to a conventional balloon. But soon they started making very specialist balloons, designed to look like the product. One of the first was a massive pair of jeans and over the years all kinds of apparitions have appeared in the skies, from motorcars to flying fire extinguishers. I recall being at a balloon festival and seeing among the great numbers of balloons taking off that a pack of canned lager was closely and appropriately being followed by oversized Alka Seltzers. It seems that almost anything can be made, as long as it has sufficient bulk – as Don Cameron said, 'We'd have problems with a bicycle.'

Balloons are now finding their place all over the world, not just owned by individuals and groups for their own amusement but increasingly as tourist attractions. What better way, for example, could you observe the wild animals of an African game reserve than floating over them in a balloon? Balloon festivals are popular and attract great crowds. The Bristol festival was founded by Don Cameron in 1979 as quite a small-scale event, but today it attracts crowds of around a hundred thousand and as many as a hundred balloons from around the world can go up in the mass ascent. Another very popular event is the nightglow. The balloons are inflated but remain on the ground, and as they light their burners they are illuminated. The whole thing is choreographed with different balloons being lit on cue to match specially chosen music.

Ballooning for fun has certainly attracted many private owners and has proved equally popular with tourists, keen to try something new but there have always been those who are looking for the next big challenge. There was no doubt among balloonists as to what that first challenge would be; fly a hot air balloon across the Atlantic. The first serious attempt was made by the pioneer of modern ballooning Ed Yost in 1976. He set off from Maine in his own balloon *Silver Fox*, travelling in a boat shaped gondola, designed to be used if the craft came down in the sea, which as it turned out was just as well. Yost chose a day when the weather forecast indicated that there would be favourable winds that would carry him towards Portugal. In the event, the forecast proved inaccurate and he discovered his course was taking him too far south and he ended up ditching the balloon without completing the crossing. He had, however, achieved a distance record of 2,740 miles. In a sense, Yost had failed but he had shown that, given the right wind conditions, an Atlantic crossing was possible. It was not long before others took up the challenge.

In 1977 Ben Arbuzzo and Maxie Anderson set off from Maine in *Double Eagle I.* Things started badly and got worse. The air currents carried them towards Mount Katahadin - at 5267 feet the highest point in Maine. Fortunately, although they came alarmingly close, they avoided contact. Then it started to snow, they were tossed up and down by a violent storm and were eventually carried so far off course that they were forced to come down in the ocean and were

Fedor Konyukhov on his solo flight round the world.

eventually picked up by helicopter. After an experience like that most people might have given up, but soon work had begun on *Double Eagle II.*

In 1978 they set off again, this time with a third pilot on board, Larry Newman. On 11 August they rose up from Presque Isle in Maine and at first things went surprisingly well for a few days. Then they hit a sudden change in atmospheric conditions and they plummeted over 9,000 feet to end up just 4,000 feet above the waves. They were saved from disaster by a bright sun that heated the gas, the envelope expanded again and they rose again to a height of almost 25,000 feet. After that alarming experience things went more smoothly and as they crossed the Irish coast, they began jettisoning unnecessary equipment, such as propane cylinders to prepare for a landing. They eventually touched down in a field of barley on 17 August, near the town of Evereux north of Paris. They had covered 3,120 miles in 137 hours.

The next big challenge was now obvious; fly right round the world. In one sense, of course, it had already been achieved, when the Arctic expedition circled the North Pole. This was not what the would-be circumnavigators had in mind. Several attempts were made, including the much-publicised attempt by Richard Branson and Peter Lindstrand in their *Virgin Global Challenger*. It became an international competition, with a substantial prize, but to claim the title of first round the world, the aeronauts had to meet conditions laid down by the World Air Sports Federation: The flight had to take place between defined latitudes, north and south of the equator, had to cross all meridians and had to cover a minimum distance of 25,000 km.

On 1 March 1999, Dr Bertrand Piccard and Brian Jones set off from Switzerland on their attempt. The balloon was a massive affair, partly hot air but also containing helium cells, built for them by Cameron Balloons in Bristol. The gondola was an egg-shaped affair made from a light carbon composite but decidedly cramped at just 11 ft by 7ft. By now, meteorology was much more exact and they were able to follow the jet streams to speed them in their way. There was a problem over the Caribbean when they began to lose speed. They decided to use some of their precious supplies of

A modern Zeppelin providing tourist trips from Friedrichshafen on Lake Constance.

propane for a long burn to carry them up to a higher altitude. At well over 30,000 feet they found the air currents they were looking for and were soon back on course and sailing along at speed. On 20 March, they crossed the last meridian. They had hoped to make a spectacular finale by landing in Egypt close to the pyramids but ended up touching down in Mauritania instead. They had more than achieved the required minimum distance, having covered a total distance of 42,810 km. In 2002, the next goal was reached when Steve Fossett became the first to make a solo flight round the world.

Having done the longest flights, the next challenge was who could go highest. The current record is held by Indian aeronaut Vjaypat Singhania, who in 2005, lifting off from Mumbai reached an altitude of 21,290 metres (69,850 feet). At the time of writing the veteran Russian adventurer Fedor Konyukhov is hoping to beat this. He is clearly a man who likes a challenge; he has already sailed round the world, rowed across the Pacific, visited both poles and has already completed a record-breaking solo round the world balloon flight. He now has two goals he is aiming to achieve: to climb the highest mountain on every continent – he's already done Everest – and to break the altitude record. Visiting the Cameron factory in Bristol, I discovered that they were already making a new balloon for this attempt. Only a really immense balloon can achieve the feat and this one will require an envelope manufactured out of a staggering 18 km of fabric. Record breaking these days is a highly technical and very expensive business.

It seemed to many that the age of the airship more or less ended with the disasters of *R101* and *Hindenburg*. Goodyear did continue to build airships in the years after the Second World War but nothing on the scale of the earlier long-distance passenger craft. Many were used mainly for promotional activities and short tourist trips. The future for more ambitious developments seemed even more bleak with the arrival of the jet airliners that made non-stop Atlantic crossing a commonplace. Anyone wanting to get from London to New York in hours rather than days would have no option; they would fly in one of the new airliners. The availability of this fast service brought the death knell to the ocean liners as far as this form of travel was concerned. But it is an undeniable fact that jetting across the Atlantic is hardly an enjoyable experience. Unless you are a first-class passenger in a Jumbo, you are stuck in a seat with little room to move, and once you are airborne, chances are that the only thing you will see out of the window is the top of the clouds you are flying high above. But there was still a market for a more enjoyable, relaxed way of travelling – not for people in a hurry but for those who wanted luxury and trips to exotic locations. The ocean liner would become the cruise ship. It seemed to some that the same scenario might work for airships.

Zeppelin are back in business with a fleet of vessels aimed specifically at the tourist market. I visited the Zeppelin museum at Friedrichshafen while looking for locations for a TV documentary series for the Discovery Channel. I was shown into the director's office and just as I walked in, a Zeppelin glided past the window. It was a magical moment and one could see the attraction of flying in it – travelling at a low altitude to get the best of the view and in comparative quiet. They currently have 12 routes in Germany and Switzerland carrying more than 20,000 passengers a year. There are plans to expand this to a worldwide service. But that is by no means the only market opening up to airships.

Over the years Lockheed have worked at developing hybrid airships specifically aimed at cargo carrying, especially to places that cannot be reached by conventional craft other than helicopters – and there are very many areas of the world where this applies. The technology uses elements from three very different types of craft. There is the conventional airship envelope to provide lift, but the design incorporates an aerodynamic element to improve performance, especially speed. And because these are craft designed to go almost anywhere and specifically to places without any official landing strips, hovercraft ideas have also been incorporated. Where the older airships had to be moored to a mast, the hybrid simply lands, cushioned by air, and able to ride easily over uneven ground. The craft has already proved its worth in its ability to, for example, deliver food to areas hit by famine. The Pioneering version built by Lockheed and Martin, *LMH1* has already been officially approved as airworthy and in 2018, Lockheed was open for business, hoping to sell the craft around the world. Apart from their versatility, the great advantage is fuel economy – and in an age of global warming, when most of the world is trying to cut down on its use of fossil fuels, this has to be an exciting development.

So now, over two centuries after the Montgolfiers astounded the world with their hot air balloon, it seems that what they began might still be open for new developments into the foreseeable future.

Select Bibliography

ABBOTT, Patrick and WAMSLEY, Nick, *British Airships in Pictures*, 1998
BECKER, Jean, *Hot Air Balloons*, 2011
CAVALLO, Tiberius, *The History and Practice of Aerostation*, 1785
CHANT, Christopher, *The Zeppelin*, 2000
COXWELL, Henry, *My Life and Balloon Experiences*, 1887-9
CROUCH, Tom D., *Lighter than Air*, 2009
ECKENER, Hugo, *My Airships* (trans,) 1958
HILDEBRANDT, A,, *Airships Past and Present*, 1908
HOLMES, Richard, *Falling Upwards*, 2011
JACKSON, Robert, *Airships*, 1971
LUNARDI, Vincent, *Accounts of First Aerial Voyage in England*, 1784
MARION, F., *Wonderful Balloon Ascents*, (trans.) 1870
NOBILE, Umberto, *My Polar Flights*, (trans.) 1961
RICHARDS, John, *A History of Airships*, 2009
ROLT, L.T.C., *The Aeronauts*, 1966
SANTOS-DUMONT, Alberto, *My Airships*, 1904
VENTRY, Lord and KOLESNIK, Eugene M., *Airship Saga*, 1982

Acknowledgements

The author would like to thank the following who have asked for acknowledgement for supplying illustrations: pp. 22, 59, Wellcome Trust; pp. 70, 75 Royal Aeronautical Society; 70, 75; Library of Congress, 83; Norwegian Museum of Science and Technology, 86; Zeppelin Museum, Friedrichshafen. 112, 177; Campbell Balloons, Bristol, 195, 196; Fedor Konyukhov

Index